NOME

"City of the Golden Beaches"

Terrence Cole, Chief Editor for this issue

Jim Walsh, Editorial Consultant

Volume 11, Number 1, 1984
ALASKA GEOGRAPHIC®

TER PHOTO
EATTLE

NOME, SHOWING MOUTH OF RIVER
BEFORE THE STORM

Table of Contents

Preface and Acknowledgments 7

Introduction 9

Chapter I . . . . . Three Lucky Swedes 10

Chapter II . . . . The Poor Man's Paradise 28

Chapter III . . . . The City on the Golden Sand . . . 42

Chapter IV . . . . On the Beach 56

Chapter V . . . . The Wickedest City 72

Chapter VI . . . . After the Gold Rush 98

Chapter VII . . . The Hardest Years 134

Chapter VIII . . . A Town that Wouldn't Die 160

Notes 178

Cover and Left — *Nome in 1900 was a sprawling city of 20,000 people, located on the edge of the Bering Sea. This view was taken from downtown Nome, looking across the Snake River to the tents on the sand spit.* (Arwine Company)

Title page — *Beyond the tent city on the beach, a fleet of ships ride at anchor in the Nome roadstead in the summer of 1900.* (Paul Mogensen and Mark Hufstetler)

The Alaska Geographic Society

To teach many more to better know and use our natural resources

(Required by 39 U.S.C. 3685)
Statement of Ownership, Management, and Circulation of *Alaska Geographic*®, a quarterly publication with home offices at Box 4-EEE, Anchorage, Alaska 99509.

Editor is Robert A. Henning. Publisher is The Alaska Geographic Society, Box 4-EEE, Anchorage, Alaska 99509. Owners are Robert A. Henning and Phyllis G. Henning, Box 4-EEE, Anchorage, Alaska 99509. Robert A. Henning and Phyllis G. Henning, husband and wife, are owners of 100 percent of all common stock outstanding.

	Average No. Copies each issue during preceding 12 months	Actual No. Copies single issue published nearest to filing date
Total No. Copies Printed	35,463	34,960
Paid Circulation		
Single Copy Sales	3,603	1,588
Mail Subscriptions	15,390	14,809
Total Paid Circulation	18,993	16,397
Free Distribution (by mail, carrier, or other means, samples, complimentary, and other free copies)	885	626
Total Distribution	19,878	17,023
Copies Not Distributed Office Use, Leftover, Unaccounted, Spoiled after printing	15,585	17,937
Return from news agencies	0	0
Total	35,463	34,960

I certify that the statements made by me above are correct and complete.
Robert A. Henning, Editor

Chief Editor: Robert A. Henning
Chief Editor this issue: Terrence Cole
Editorial Consultant: Jim Walsh
Editor: Penny Rennick
Editorial Assistant: Kathy Doogan
Production Editor: Warren Ernst
Art Director: Sandra Harner
Designer: Roselyn Pape

ALASKA GEOGRAPHIC®, ISSN 0361-1353, is published quarterly by The Alaska Geographic Society, Anchorage, Alaska 99509-6057. Second-class postage paid in Edmonds, Washington 98020-3588. Printed in U.S.A.

THE ALASKA GEOGRAPHIC SOCIETY is a nonprofit organization exploring new frontiers of knowledge across the lands of the polar rim, learning how other men and other countries live in their Norths, putting the geography book back in the classroom, exploring new methods of teaching and learning — sharing in the excitement of discovery in man's wonderful new world north of 51°16′.

MEMBERS OF THE SOCIETY RECEIVE *Alaska Geographic*®, a quality magazine which devotes each quarterly issue to monographic in-depth coverage of a northern geographic region or resource-oriented subject.

MEMBERSHIP DUES in The Alaska Geographic Society are $30 per year; $34 to non-U.S. addresses. (Eighty percent of each year's dues is for a one-year subscription to *Alaska Geographic*®.) Order from The Alaska Geographic Society, Box 4-EEE, Anchorage, Alaska 99509-6057; (907) 274-0521.

MATERIAL SOUGHT: The editors of *Alaska Geographic*® seek a wide variety of informative material on the lands north of 51°16′ on geographic subjects — anything to do with resources and their uses (with heavy emphasis on quality color photography) — from Alaska, northern Canada, Siberia, Japan — all geographic areas that have a relationship to Alaska in a physical or economic sense. We do not want material done in excessive scientific terminology. A query to the editors is suggested. Payments are made for all material upon publication.

CHANGE OF ADDRESS: The post office does not automatically forward *Alaska Geographic*® when you move. To ensure continous service, notify us six weeks before moving. Send us your new address and zip code (and moving date), your old address and zip code, and if possible send a mailing label from a copy of *Alaska Geographic*®. Send this information to *Alaska Geographic*® Mailing Offices, 130 Second Avenue South, Edmonds, Washington 98020-3588.

MAILING LISTS: We have begun making our members' names and addresses available to carefully screened publications and companies whose products and activities might be of interest to you. If you would prefer not to receive such mailings, please so advise us, and include your mailing label (or your name and address if label is not available).

Library of Congress cataloging in publication data:
Cole, Terrence, 1953—
  Nome, city of the golden beaches.

(Alaska geographic ; v. 11, no.1)
Bibliography: p.
  1. Nome (Alaska)—History.   I. Title.   II. Series.
F901.A266   vol. 11, no. 1   [F914.N6]   979.8'4 84-294
ISBN 0-88240-201-3

Three Seward Peninsula miners and their bags of gold dust in 1906. (Bancroft Library)

Preface and Acknowledgments

The story of Nome, like that of so many other Alaskan towns, is closely intertwined with the history of the Klondike. Yet the Klondike River and the gold district named for it are not in Alaska as is commonly believed, but in Yukon Territory, Canada. The real Alaska gold rush was not to the Klondike in 1898, but to the sandy beaches at Nome a thousand miles to the west in the summer of 1900.

Despite the huge volume of material written about Nome in the last 80 years, there has never been a comprehensive history of Alaska's greatest gold rush town. Few historians have ever delved very deeply into the wild story of the Nome stampede and one of the most unusual gold strikes in history.

When miners found gold in the sand on the Nome beach, many presumed that the gold had been washed ashore by the waves and had come in with the tide like driftwood. Across the United States fortune hunters envisioned the Bering Sea as a golden lake, from which an inexhaustible supply of treasure could be dredged. No less improbable was the strange town that grew up on the shores of the golden sea, and is still there today.

Many people have been of great help during the five years that I've spent researching and writing about the history of Nome. Materials have been gathered from many libraries and archives, ranging from the Carrie McLain Museum on the wind-swept beach at Nome to the National Archives on the equally cold and wind-swept streets of Washington, D.C., in December.

Among the many individuals who provided information, photographs, or other assistance, I would especially like to thank: Michael Allen, Kevin Cole, Dermot Cole, Roy Johnson, Renee Blahuta, Diane Brenner, Kent Sturgis, Phyllis DeMuth, William Roberts, Georgeen Klassen, Mark Hufstetler, Paul Mogensen, Carl B. Lancaster, Thomas McGinn Smith, Walter Marx, Lyman Woodman, Alice Osborne, Virginia McKinney, Earl Beistline, Howard Hein, Beth Hunt, Dexter S. Bartlett, Dave Nelson, Evangeline Atwood, William Hanable, Joan M. Antonson, Robert W. Stevens, James H. Ducker, Mary Mangusso, Carol Zabilski, Carl Solberg, Scott Lytle, Aldon Bell, Glenda Pearson, Lea Ehrlich, Bob Bjoring, Susan Cunningham, Carla Rickerson, Ethel Becker, John Haile Cloe, Leta Hamilton, Tom and Larry Martin, Jim Moody, Sandra Harner, Roz Pape, Norm Bolotin, and Warren Ernst.

Bob Henning, the President of The Alaska Geographic Society, has provided continual support and encouragement. Jim Walsh, who was born and raised in Nome, and whose family has lived on the Bering Sea since the gold rush, provided many special insights into the history of his home town. Dr. Robert E. Burke, who directed my Ph.D. dissertation at the University of Washington, for which some of this research was first done, acted as both an editor and a friend.

I have been fortunate to have had advice and suggestions from some of the foremost experts on Alaskan history, including Leland Carlson, William Wilson, Morgan Sherwood, Robert N. De Armond, William R. Hunt, Claus-M. Naske, and Dorothy Jean Ray.

Finally I would like to say thank-you to my wife, Marjorie, and to my father and mother, William P. and Anne E. Cole.

Terrence Cole

Ice jams in front of Nome at the mouth of the Snake River, May 22, 1907.
(National Maritime Museum)

Introduction

No other place in the world is quite like Nome, the most famous gold rush town in Alaska. Thousands of people landed on the Nome beach in the space of a few weeks in the summer of 1900 looking for gold. It was the last major placer gold stampede in the history of the American West, and Nome was one of the last great gold rush boom towns. The stampede lasted only for one short summer, but the town survived and has become the major mining and supply center for northwestern Alaska.

Nome now has a population of about three thousand people. For years it has been proposed that a road be built to Nome from Fairbanks or from another spot in the Interior, but as of now Nome is accessible only by boat, plane, or dog sled. The town is icebound for more than six months each year, and Nome has no harbor in which ships can ride out the storms that roll in off the Bering Sea, a problem that has plagued the city since the gold rush. In the past the city itself has been nearly blown away by the savage sea storms, and after World War II the Army Corps of Engineers built a million-dollar granite sea wall along the beach to save the town from washing into the surf. On several other occasions the city was almost completely destroyed by fire. Yet Nome is a gold rush town that would not die, and each time it has come back.

Many people believe that Nome will someday boom again; if a road is built to Fairbanks, if offshore oil development is promoted, or if the gold mining industry revives. Others hope to preserve the old flavor of the gold rush town, and are content with the fact that Nome's golden days were more than 80 years ago. There was vocal opposition to the paving of Nome's main street in the early 1970s by those who were sad to see the dirt streets and wooden sidewalks give way to progress.

The modern-day city of Nome is but a ghost of what it once was. At its height in 1900 Nome was about 10 times the size it is today. The city appeared overnight on the frozen tundra, about one hundred miles from the nearest tree, and more than two thousand miles north of Seattle. Many people thought it was the most desolate place on earth, but within months the early prospectors' campsite at the mouth of the Snake River became a city of close to 20,000 people, with congested streets and ferocious traffic jams, steam-heated hotels, beer gardens, several newspapers, wooden-planked streets, a railroad, theaters, and about one hundred saloons and gambling houses.

The instant city on the Bering Sea attracted a strange collection of gold seekers and fortune hunters. They came from all over the world with dreams of striking it rich on the Nome beach, where gold had been discovered in the sand along the seashore.

Most of the stampeders who landed on the Nome beach in 1900 stayed only a few months. Hundreds went home dead broke, and the government had to send them back to Seattle on army transports like wartime refugees. But others stuck it out and some families have been in Nome now for four generations. All are part of the story of Nome, the town that was justly described in 1900 as "the strangest community ever seen upon the face of this old earth."[1]

Two bicyclists cruising past the crowds of sidewalk miners on Front Street in Nome.
(Museum of History and Industry)

"The Klondike Fever"
"Willamette" leaving Seattle
with 800 Passengers

Wilson
Seattle

Chapter I
Three Lucky Swedes

When word of George Carmack's discovery of gold on the Klondike River reached the West Coast in 1897, it touched off a stampede that would change forever the history of Alaska. The first ship to reach the United States with the treasure from the Klondike was the *Excelsior,* which docked at San Francisco on July 15, 1897. Two days later the *Portland* reached Seattle with a second load of men carrying bags of gold dust and nuggets that ranged "from the size of a pea to a guinea egg."[1]

"The stories they tell seem too incredulous and far beyond belief," the *Seattle Post-Intelligencer* reported. Most of the men had not had any previous experience at mining, and yet they were returning as wealthy men. Some of them were millionaires. "They all have gold," a reporter who visited the *Portland* wrote, "and it is piled about the staterooms like so much valueless hand baggage."[2] Few of the men carried less than $5,000 in gold down the gangplank with them, and some had more than $100,000 in their trunks and boxes. Altogether the ship was loaded with nearly two tons of Klondike gold.

Daniel B. Libby of California was unique among the thousands of men who quit their jobs, abandoned their careers, or came out of retirement in 1897 and 1898 to go to the northern gold fields. Almost immediately after the first shipment of Klondike gold reached San Francisco, Libby mounted an expedition to an isolated area on the Seward Peninsula, about a thousand miles west of the Klondike. It was no wild goose chase, because 30 years earlier Libby had spent a winter in northwestern Alaska, and he believed that he had once discovered gold in that far-off country. Daniel Libby thought about the traces of gold he had seen in an Alaskan stream from time to time, but never seriously until 1897, when he joined the stampede to the north hoping he could find the stream again before someone else did.

Libby had first discovered signs of gold in Alaska in the 1860s when he was working on a project that could have been invented by Jules Verne, a round-the-world telegraph line. Several unsuccessful attempts had been made in the 1850s to lay an underwater telegraph cable across the Atlantic Ocean, and it was generally believed that transoceanic submarine cables were impractical. Thus was born the idea of tying the continents together by an overland telegraph line from the United States to Europe across the Bering Strait. In 1864 the Western Union telegraph company raised the capital necessary to finance five thousand miles of telegraph line from a point "not east of Chicago" to the mouth of the Amur River in Siberia. It was a daring venture. The proposed route lay across one of the greatest expanses of unexplored wilderness in the world, through western Canada, Russian America, and Siberia. The first transcontinental line in the United States from the East Coast to San Francisco had been completed only three years earlier in 1861, and many people believed that another five thousand miles of telegraph line could be built through the Arctic. "We hold the ball of the earth in our hand," a proponent of the round-the-world telegraph said in the early 1860s, "and wind upon it a network of living and thinking wire. . . ."[3]

Advance parties were sent out to various spots along the route to begin construction in 1865 and 1866, including a group led by Daniel B. Libby, a young Civil War veteran from the state of Maine. On September 16, 1866, Captain Libby and his crew of about 40 men arrived

Stampeders bound for the Klondike in 1897. (University of Washington Library)

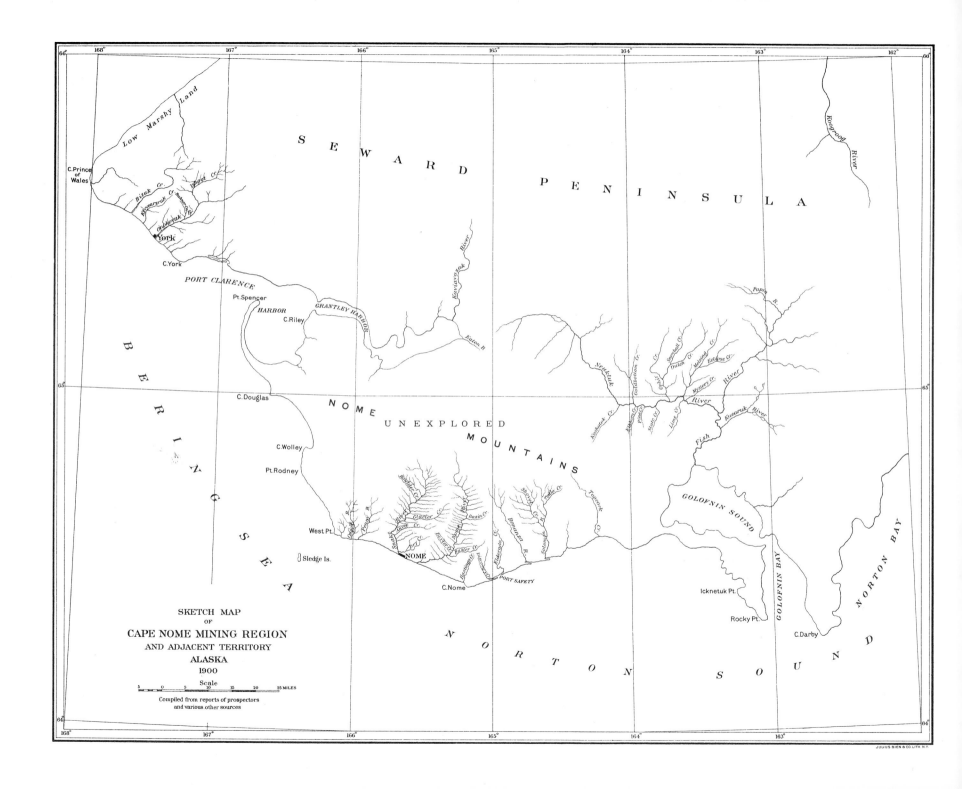

SKETCH MAP
OF
CAPE NOME MINING REGION
AND ADJACENT TERRITORY
ALASKA
1900

Scale

Compiled from reports of prospectors
and various other sources

at Port Clarence, near Grantley Harbor, Russian America, on the eastern side of the Bering Strait. The telegraph crew dubbed their camp Libbysville in honor of their 22-year-old leader, and also perhaps in honor of the infamous Confederate prison of the same name. After the company's supply ships sailed south in the fall, the men at Libbysville were completely isolated, locked in their own arctic prison for the next 10 months.

The winter of 1866-67 was a long cold one at Libbysville. The men were poorly equipped for arctic conditions. They had been supplied with blue sack coats, which were almost useless in a land where the temperature could drop to 70° below zero. In general their clothing was too small, cheaply made, and in short supply, and their tents gave little protection against the wind.

The job of Libby's crew was crew to build a section of the telegraph line several hundred miles across the unexplored wilderness now called the Seward Peninsula. While completing the first part of the line to the head of Grantley Harbor, Libby was worried that some of his men would freeze to death. "While we were doing this work we experienced terrible cold and stormy weather," he reported, "and the thermometer fell to fifty-five degrees below zero. Great was my anxiety for my men camping in common tents as some of them were, but fortunately, none were frozen."[4]

While waiting for the long winter to end, the men at Libbysville did the best they could to entertain themselves. On the first Sunday of every month they published a handwritten newspaper called the *Esquimaux* edited by J.J. Harrington, one of the men in Libby's crew. The editor boasted that the *Esquimaux* was the only periodical published on the globe between China on the one hand, and Victoria, British Columbia, on the other. Libbysville had a library with 50 books, and editorials in the *Esquimaux* regularly warned the men to read and to spend their time constructively, "when the stormy weather keeps us in doors, and the long nights make the hours hang heavy on our hands."[5]

The 40 men at Libbysville greeted New Year's Day, 1867, and wondered a great deal about what had happened in the outside world since they had left California in July. They had not received any reliable news in six months, and would not get any for probably another six months more. They were curious to know if the war between Austria and Prussia was over, or if Jefferson Davis had been brought to trial for treason. As editor Harrington wrote, "We are actually outside of the world." One disconcerting rumor that had reached Libbysville was that the Atlantic cable had been successfully laid in the summer of 1866. The *Esquimaux*, however, doubted the story, and said that this was "an unlooked for event."[6]

Of much more immediate concern was the fact that by April 1867, Libbysville had run out of food. All work stopped on the telegraph line, and Libby explained, "we could do no more but return and patiently wait the coming of the vessels." So his men would not starve to death he sent everyone out in different directions to hunt and fish for themselves. "It was with great difficulty that they got enough to eat," he said, "and sometimes I have known them to go hungry." Their only thought was that one of the telegraph company's ships would arrive quickly with supplies, and Libby admitted, "We lived and dragged along with the hope of being soon relieved by one of the Company's vessels."[7]

The disastrous winter for the men at Libbysville finally ended on June 28, 1867, when the first supply ship of the season arrived with the news that the Atlantic cable had been in operation for nearly a year, and that the overland telegraph project had been officially abandoned four months earlier. The Western Union party sailed away from Libbysville on July 2, 1867, never to return. Anything that was portable was shipped to San Francisco, and the rest was left behind, including the 23 miles of telegraph line that they had strung across the tundra. On the front of one of the buildings the men painted the words, "Libby Station. Established September 17, 1866.

At the time of the Nome gold rush most of the Seward Peninsula was unmapped and unexplored, as this 1900 U.S. Geological Survey map illustrates. The proposed route of the Western Union Telegraph line in the 1860s was across the peninsula from the head of Grantley Harbor down the Niukluk and Fish rivers to Golovin Bay. While surveying this route, Daniel Libby discovered gold in the valley of the Fish River.
(U.S. Geological Survey)

Vacated July 2, 1867." Inside they posted a notice which explained the history of the project. The sign named the two men buried "beneath the frozen sod" who had died over the winter, and listed the names of all who had been there, so that if white men came again to those desolate shores, they might know of those who had gone before them.[8]

Forty years later some of the telegraph poles erected by Libby and his men were still standing on the Seward Peninsula. But there was another legacy to the future from the great scheme to build a round-the-world telegraph line besides the rotting telegraph poles in the tundra. Libby had twice personally surveyed the entire two-hundred-mile-long route over which the telegraph line was to pass in his district. He had found a good route north from Golovin Bay up the valley of the Fish and Niukluk rivers, crossing a portage at the head of the Niukluk to what was later named the Pilgrim River, and continuing northwest to Port Clarence. On one of his surveys over the route Libby and another man working for Western Union, Baron Otto Von Bendeleben, saw "unmistakable evidence" of the presence of placer gold in the valley of the Fish River, and on other streams between Port Clarence and Golovin Bay.[9] Libby intended to return to the creeks to prospect the ground more carefully, but when Western Union abandoned the telegraph line, he gave up the idea of going back to look for gold.

After leaving Alaska in 1867 Libby moved to San Francisco. For 30 years he kept the notes and maps he had made in the Arctic, often talking idly of going back someday. But nothing ever came of it until after the discovery of the millions of dollars of gold in the Klondike. Only then did he realize that he might have stumbled across a bonanza in 1867, and never knew it.

Within a few weeks of the arrival in San Francisco of the first gold from the Klondike, Libby had organized an expedition to search for the stream he had seen 30 years earlier in Alaska. He picked three partners to go

with him, including his brother-in-law Louis Melsing, H.L. Blake, a mining engineer, and A.P. Mordaunt. Several San Francisco capitalists underwrote the cost of the expedition, and Libby purchased enough supplies and provisions to last the four-man party for several years. On August 18, 1897, they left San Francisco on board the steamer North Fork, bound for Golovin Bay.[10]

"I don't suppose you will hear from me again for at least ten months," Louis Melsing wrote his sister on the trip north, "so I will wish you and all the folks a pleasant Thanksgiving, a Merry Christmas, and a Happy New Year, and, perhaps a noisy Fourth of July."[11] By that time Libby, Melsing, Blake and Mordaunt had found the gold they were looking for, in a river valley which Daniel Libby had first seen in 1866.

In the years since Libby had worked on the Western Union telegraph project, other prospectors had reported the presence of various minerals, including gold, silver, and galena, on the Seward Peninsula. In the early 1880s local Natives had shown whalers in Golovin Bay samples of silver ore from Omilak Mountain near Fish River and the discovery led to the creation of the first mining district on the Seward Peninsula. The Omilak silver mine never became a profitable operation, despite the attempts of several promoters to develop it.[12] Yet the silver mine brought other prospectors and traders into the area, including John A. Dexter.

Dexter was an old seafaring man and Bering Sea whaler, who had once worked at the Omilak silver mine. He thought he liked the northwest coast of Alaska as much as any other place he had seen in the world, and decided to stay on the Seward Peninsula. He founded a trading post at Cheenik on Golovin Bay in 1892, which became the most important trading center for the region. He was the best-known trader on the coast, and traveled widely throughout northwestern Alaska.

When Daniel Libby and his three partners arrived at Dexter's Trading Post at Golovin Bay in the fall of 1897, they learned that they were not the only men who hoped

The early prospectors on the treeless coast of the Bering Sea often built their cabins out of driftwood. (Museum of History and Industry)

Eskimo cooking Walrus Meat.

THE NATIVES

Since time immemorial Eskimos have lived in the area around Bering Strait. When prospectors overran the Seward Peninsula at the turn of the century, they found a people who had had their first contact with Europeans 250 years earlier, and had learned many of the white man's ways. But the Eskimos had never seen anything quite like the crazy stampede to Nome in 1900. **Left** *— A family cooking walrus meat on the Nome waterfront. Natives often camped on the beach near Nome during the summertime, after traveling hundreds of miles across the ocean in their umiaks or kayaks, like this group (below) of East Cape Eskimos from Siberia.* **Right** *— A mother and her baby.*

EAST CAPE ESKIMO ARRIVING IN NOME, ALASKA

D.S. Bartlett

"Siberian Eskimo Mother & Child."

BEACH SALOON
NOLAN & RICHARDSON

RIVER FRONT COUNCIL

BEACH COUNCIL

to strike it rich on the Seward Peninsula. Dexter showed Libby samples of gold found in the region, and told the newcomers about the creeks which would be the most likely areas to prospect.

In addition, N.O. Hultberg, a Swedish missionary at Cheenik who had done some prospecting in the area, and the mission teacher P.H. Anderson, had caught the gold fever. So had Dr. A.N. Kittilsen, a government physician who was assistant superintendent of the reindeer station at Port Clarence. All of these men would play key roles in the bitter history of the discovery of the Nome gold fields, and afterward most of them hated one another.

Even today the story of the gold discovery at Nome is not totally clear. There are many contradictory accounts and it is hard to sift fact from fiction. It was not much easier at the turn of the century. More than 80 years ago, on January 1, 1900, the first edition of the *Nome Nugget* asked in a front page headline, "WHO DISCOVERED NOME?" There were so many different stories of the discovery that the newspaper could not determine who should get the credit for making the gold strike. Instead the *Nugget* decided to print several different versions of the beginning of Nome, and leave "future historians to settle the dispute."[13]

Some facts are known for certain. On April 23, 1898, the Libby party made the first major gold strike on the Seward Peninsula, on streams they called Melsing Creek and Ophir Creek. Following the tradition that had been established in the early days in the California gold fields, Libby, Blake, Melsing, and Mordaunt, as well as the two Swedish missionaries from Cheenik, Hultberg and Anderson, and the government physician, Dr. Kittilsen, officially called a miners' meeting and organized a mining district. Libby, Blake, and Melsing also staked a 240-acre townsite on the Niukluk River near the mouth of Melsing Creek, and called it Council City, in honor of the council, or miners' meeting, they had held there.[14]

Council City was the first permanently settled placer gold mining camp on the Seward Peninsula, and the region produced nearly $12 million in gold over the next 30 years.[15] But the Council City strike was the prelude to a far richer discovery made about 80 miles to the west six months later near Cape Nome.

The men generally credited with the discovery of the Nome gold fields are Jafet Lindeberg, Eric Lindblom, and John Brynteson, the "three lucky Swedes." However, H.L. Blake of the Libby party claimed that as early as Christmas 1897, he had found gold on Anvil Creek in the Nome district, one of the richest gold-bearing streams ever discovered in Alaska.[16] That contention seems highly unlikely. But in the summer of 1898, Blake, the Swedish missionary Rev. Nels O. Hultberg, and four other companions including John Brynteson, a Swedish coal miner from northern Michigan, were traveling westward along the coast of the Seward Peninsula in a small boat, when a violent storm forced them to head for shore. They attempted to take cover inside the mouth of a winding stream, but their boat swamped in the breakers just as they entered the river, and most of their supplies were lost in the surf.

It had been an ill-fated expedition from the start. Blake and Hultberg had been fighting almost constantly since the party had left Golovin Bay on July 31. The seasick miners were glad to be on firm ground again, but their dispositions did not improve. The next morning they had to wash down their pancakes with cold water, because all of their coffee had been lost in the surf.

Worst of all, these six weary prospectors had landed in a valley where there there was more gold than they could have spent in a lifetime, but they did not find it. The storm had blown them ashore at the mouth of the Snake River, where the three lucky Swedes landed about six weeks later and staked the claims that made them millionaires.

Hultberg and Blake were so busy arguing that they had little time to look for gold. Hultberg reportedly did find excellent prospects on a tributary of the Snake

Council City on the Niukluk River, the first gold mining town on the Seward Peninsula. (Ethel Becker)

River, which was later called Anvil Creek, but he never told his partner. "Dey is not any gold up dare," Blake said Hultberg told him, mimicking the missionary's thick Swedish accent.[17] After a few cursory prospecting trips, the six men continued to the west when the storm subsided, leaving the richest valley in northwestern Alaska without staking a single claim.

The men who did stake the first claims in the Snake River valley were not the veteran prospectors of legend who had spent their lives searching for gold. When they made their famous discovery in September 1898, Jafet Lindeberg, Eric Lindblom, and John Brynteson each had about two months' experience at prospecting, and none of them knew much about gold mining. They had met by accident at Council City in August 1898, and became partners. One month later the three greenhorns struck it rich.

Eric Lindblom was 41 years old in 1898, and was the oldest of the trio. He was born in Sweden in 1857, and

had traveled over much of Europe plying his trade as a tailor before he came to the United States in 1886. Lindblom was living in Oakland, California, when the first shipments of gold arrived from the Klondike, and he decided to join the stampede north. However, he did not have the price of a ticket, and signed on as a deck hand on a whaling ship. Some accounts state that Lindblom was actually shanghaied while drunk in San Francisco, and woke up with a headache one morning to find himself on his way to Kotzebue Sound. Others say that he did not understand English very well, and unintentionally signed up for a two-year hitch on a whaler. Either way, in the spring of 1898, the little Swedish tailor was working before the mast on a ship bound for the Bering Sea.

Lindblom apparently planned to desert the ship when it reached Kotzebue Sound, where gold had reportedly been found in the Kobuk River valley. But on the way north, Lindblom heard rumors of the Libby party's gold strike on Ophir Creek, and he decided to desert the whaler as soon as possible, and to head for the Council City district. While his ship was stopped at Grantley Harbor waiting for the ice in the Bering Strait to clear so that the ship could safely sail through to Kotzebue Sound, Lindblom was sent ashore to fetch fresh water. He never came back.

For several days the little Swedish tailor eluded search parties sent out to find him, but he had nothing to eat and was soon exhausted. He had no idea of how to live in the wilderness and had assumed that he could easily walk the more than one hundred miles across the tundra to the Council City district without any food or other supplies. After three days as a fugitive he met a lone prospector who told him to go back to his ship because "his bones would bleach in the mountains if he persisted in the attempt to cross the country to Golovin Bay."[18]

Lindblom returned to Grantley Harbor and found an Eskimo family about to start on a trading expedition to Golovin Bay. When the Eskimo boat headed out of the harbor it passed within a few dozen feet of Lindblom's old ship, with Lindblom hiding inside underneath a pile of animal pelts. He wasn't seen, as one account explains, "but he nearly died of suffocation, and the stench of the skins made him dreadfully sick." When his old shipmates were safely out of sight, "Mr. Lindblom thankfully breathed the pure air again."[19]

On his trip along the coast Lindblom said that his Eskimo hosts stopped to fish at the mouth of the Snake River. While they were fishing he claimed to have found gold in several tributaries of the river, and that therefore he was the first man to find gold in the Nome district.[20]

Lindblom arrived at John Dexter's trading post in late July 1898, and allegedly he told Rev. Nels O. Hultberg that there was gold in the Snake River valley. A short time later Hultberg left on the dissent-ridden prospecting trip he took along the coast with H.L. Blake. And one of Hultberg's companions on that expedition was John Brynteson, the second member of the lucky Swedes.

Brynteson had emigrated to the United States from

The first prospectors in the Nome district, including the "three lucky Swedes," 1-Jafet Lindeberg, 2-John Brynteson, 3-Eric Lindblom. (University of Washington Library)

A lone prospector trudging across the tundra. (Denny Collection, University of Alaska Archives)

was a 24-year-old Norwegian, who came to the United States as a government reindeer herder, but his real goal was to earn his passage to the Alaska gold fields.

At the time of the Klondike gold rush the United States government sent an expedition to Lapland to purchase reindeer and to ship them to Alaska, with the idea of using the deer to haul supplies to the miners in Dawson City, many of whom it was feared would starve without government assistance. One of the men that the American government recruited to herd the deer was Jafet Lindeberg, whose home was along a fjord in northernmost Scandinavia, where the local industries were lumbering, fishing, and dairying. "I never had anything to do with reindeer," Lindeberg said later, but he was eager to get to the gold fields any way that he could.[22] He signed up as a herder, and in December 1897 left for the United States on a ship with more than five hundred reindeer.

The Klondike reindeer project was a fiasco from the start, and most of the deer starved to death long before they reached Dawson City. For Lindeberg however, the reindeer expedition was his ticket to fortune. After working for a time with the herd destined for Dawson City, and actually leaving the government service for a short time, he was reassigned to Plover Bay, Siberia, where he was to trade with the local natives for Siberian reindeer. When he reached Saint Michael, Lindeberg learned that the Siberian natives had driven away the man whom he was going to relieve at Plover Bay, and the plan was abandoned. Lindeberg resigned his position for good, and became a prospector.

At first Lindeberg intended to go to the Klondike along with almost everyone else in the summer of 1898, but he had met Dr. A.N. Kittilsen, the government physician of the reindeer service and a fellow Norwegian. Kittilsen was one of the seven men who had organized the first mining district at Council City a few months earlier, and he urged Lindeberg to investigate the gold discoveries in the Council district. The former reindeer herder arrived

Sweden at the age of 16 in 1887. Like Lindblom he had known hard times. He had worked in the iron and coal mines of northern Michigan for seven years before leaving for Alaska in 1898. At the suggestion of a Swedish missionary colleague of Rev. Nels O. Hultberg, Brynteson had come to Alaska to prospect for coal.[21] Of the three original discoverers of the Nome gold fields, he was the only experienced miner.

Bryteson and Lindblom were both naturalized American citizens, but the last and the youngest of the three Swedes had just arrived in the United States in January 1898 from northern Norway. Jafet Lindeberg

at Council City in August 1898, where he soon met two other greenhorn miners who had just arrived in the country, Eric Lindblom and John Brynteson.

"We three men met by chance at Council City in August, 1898," Lindeberg said. None of them knew much about gold mining, but all three realized that they had to prospect in a new region because by the late summer of 1898 the Council City district was "overrun by stampeders, and staked to the mountain tops."[23]

In early September of 1898, Lindeberg, Lindblom, and Brynteson patched up an old flat-bottomed scow and sailed west from Dexter's Trading Post at Cheenik. They were bound for the river valley about one hundred miles to the west, where several prospectors claimed to have seen signs of gold, although no one as yet had staked a single claim. After several days of battling stormy weather in their makeshift boat, they came ashore at the mouth of the winding stream which they called the Snake River. Within a week the three greenhorns, who supposedly could not tell a "placer from a potato patch," had staked most of the best claims in one of the richest gold fields ever found in Alaska.[24]

They struck gold in "paying quantities" on about a half-dozen tributaries of the Snake River, all of which they named, including Anvil Creek, Snow Gulch, Glacier Creek, Rock Creek, and Dry Creek. By far the richest of all was Anvil Creek, which they named for a large anvil-shaped rock that stands on a mountain above the stream.[25]

After staking claims on the creeks they had discovered, the three Swedes returned to Dexter's Trading Post, with a shotgun shell full of gold dust.

They kept their find a secret, and only told a few fellow Scandinavians of their discovery. It was fortunate for them, because neither Lindeberg, Brynteson, nor Lindblom knew the proper procedures for locating and recording a mining claim. Their claims were not the correct size, and they had not been marked properly. They had not held a miners' meeting to organize a mining

Anvil Rock on Anvil Mountain outside of Nome. (Powell Collection, University of Alaska Archives)

district, nor appointed a recorder who could officially record the claims. Until those steps were taken, their mining claims were not legally valid.

The veteran miner that they invited to go back with them so they could stake their claims correctly was Gabe W. Price from California. Price was an agent of Charles D. Lane, a multimillionaire miner and investor from San Francisco, and he knew the intricacies of mining law. By tradition at least a half-dozen men were needed to call a miners' meeting, and so Dr. Kittilsen, and a Lapp reindeer herder, J.S. Tornanses, were also invited to accompany Lindeberg, Lindblom, and Brynteson back

Riding his favorite horse is Gabe Price, the man who organized the Cape Nome Mining District in the fall of 1898. (Paul Mogensen and Mark Hufstetler)

of my claim in one day with one rocker, and $1800 in five days with two rockers."[27] Price was a happy man when he wrote letters to his wife and to his boss, Charles D. Lane in San Francisco, telling them of his good fortune. He estimated that his claim on Anvil Creek, No. 8 Above Discovery, would produce $100,000 the next year. Charles Lane said that when he received this letter from Price, he began to organize a company that he wryly called the Wild Goose Mining and Trading Company. Though Lane had earlier been disappointed in a mining venture in Kotzebue Sound, this time he was not on a wild goose chase. His company became the largest mining corporation in northwestern Alaska.[28]

As word of the discovery spread, miners from the Council City district poured into the area. Many of the Council City miners were eager to believe that the claims staked by the original locators were illegal. The general feeling was that no greenhorns, especially Swedes, could or should have been so lucky. Some charged that the Swedes were not American citizens and were therefore not eligible to locate mining claims, and that the Scandinavians had staked many claims by power of attorney for their friends and countrymen which were not valid. H.L. Blake was bitter, because he maintained that he was the real discoverer of the Nome gold fields, and that the missionaries and greenhorns had cheated him. Libby, Melsing, and Mordaunt were also angry that the Swedes had not shared their secret, because Anderson, Kittilsen, and Hultberg had all been privy to the Libby party's strike at Council in the spring.

The belief that aliens had conspired to cheat true-blue American miners out of their heritage and their bank accounts started a massive tidal wave of claim jumping and reckless staking by power of attorney. Newcomers automatically jumped every claim, as Rex Beach phrased it, "whose location notice bore a name ending in 'son,' 'berg,' or had three consonants in a row."[29] Speculators also blanketed the district with mining claims, often without touching the ground with a pick or shovel. By the spring

to the scene of the strike in early October 1898. On October 15, the six men officially organized the Cape Nome Mining District, and under the watchful eye of Gabe Price all of the claims were carefully staked and measured.

Winter was approaching quickly and the streams had already started to freeze over. But in about five days' time, with the use of two crude wooden rockers and heated water to soften the frozen ground, they rocked out nearly $2,000 from Snow Gulch and Anvil Creek. This was the first gold produced at Nome.[26]

At first the six men planned to keep their discovery a secret, but that proved to be impossible. In mid-November Gabe Price wrote a friend at Council City urging him to leave for the new gold camp of Nome City at the mouth of the Snake River. "Do not make this known too much," Price wrote, "but we took $352.60 out

of 1899 the few hundred men in the Nome district had staked about fifteen hundred mining claims, which were enough if placed end to end, as one observer pointed out, to stretch the entire length of the state of Illinois.[30]

After navigation opened in the Bering Sea in 1899, a new swarm of prospectors arrived in the Nome district, swelling the population to almost three thousand by early July. Many of the new arrivals were from the Yukon valley, but a large number came from Kotzebue Sound and the Kobuk River valley north of the Seward Penin-sula. Hundreds of men had rushed to Kotzebue Sound in 1898 only to find themselves icebound for the winter in a place where there was no gold. By the summer of 1899 most of the Kotzebue Sound stampeders were destitute, and they waited to be rescued by a government revenue cutter and taken back to civilization. Several hundred of these destitutes made their way to the Nome district where they found a camp choked with speculators, and a huge throng of other luckless men from the Yukon.

One of the first pictures taken of the tent city of Nome. (Bancroft Library)

Looking west from Lane Way

Street in Nome

Of the estimated three thousand men at Nome in July 1899, about one thousand were destitute.[31] Most of them put up their tents on the Nome beach, in between the piles of driftwood, as that was the only unclaimed space available to them near the townsite at the mouth of the Snake River. They were the dregs of the Klondike stampede, those who had bet everything on striking it rich, and had lost it all. The Scandinavians and other alleged aliens in the district were natural scapegoats, and claim jumping, which had been going on all winter, became an absolute mania. In the first three weeks after navigation opened for the year in mid-June, almost every potentially valuable claim in the Nome district was jumped at least twice, and some claims were located by more than a half-dozen jumpers.[32]

Claim jumping was often little more than ritualized blackmail, as the true owner would often rather pay off rival claimants to a piece of mining ground than to have the property tied up for years in legal challenges. In Nome, however, the mass jumping mania was leading to anarchy, and the camp almost exploded into violence on the night of July 10, 1899. On that evening a miners' meeting of five hundred to six hundred men was called to order in the large tent of the Northern Saloon, intending to declare all of the existing mining locations in the Nome district void and illegal, and to reopen all of the creeks for staking. At the same time other men were stationed on Anvil Mountain about four miles away, waiting for a bonfire to be lit that would signal the passage of the resolutions voiding the claims of the Swedes and the other original stakers. Once the men on Anvil Mountain received the signal they would race to relocate for themselves and their partners all of the best claims in the district.[33]

It was a daring plan and was foiled only by the quick action of Lieutenant O.L. Spaulding of the U.S. Army. Lieutenant Spaulding and about a half-dozen soldiers forced the meeting to disperse at bayonet point, and the military warned the "agitators" that further acts which might incite bloodshed, or "meetings held with the obvious intention to cause disorder, at which incendiary and menacing speech was permitted, would not be tolerated."[34]

While claim owners applauded the measures taken by the army to preserve order, most of the men in the camp without mining claims were outraged and charged that the army's actions were an "unwarranted interference with the American right of free speech."[35] The situation grew more menacing and dangerous each day. To prevent bloodshed the army forbade anyone to carry firearms, revolvers or pistols.

For the destitute men camped on the beach, or those hanging around the saloons complaining about the lack of opportunity for an honest man in Nome, their great dreams of striking it rich on the 1898 stampede seemed to have finally come to an inglorious end. Within a few days, however, a remarkable change had taken place. The disappointed men had deserted the saloons and gambling tables. Even the barkeepers and the faro dealers were gone it was said, "leaving a single man on watch to quench the thirst of the casual customer."[36] Barbers and lawyers closed up their shops; and those men who had paying jobs on the creeks quit them gleefully, delighted that they did not have to listen to the mine boss anymore, though some of the bosses walked off the job too. Gone also were the few women and children in the camp, because on the sandy beach in front of Nome, a near miraculous discovery had been made.

There was gold in the sand. The Nome beach was so rich that a man could almost pick gold up off the beach like sea shells or driftwood. The miners called it "the poor man's paradise."

Looking west down Nome's Front Street in 1899. (Lulu Fairbanks Collection, University of Alaska Archives)

Digging for gold on the Nome beach with a shovel, a rocker, and a handmade wheelbarrow. (Ethel Becker)

Chapter II
The Poor Man's Paradise

It has grown as if by magic," Nome's first newspaper bragged about the town in its first issue. "It is true it is built upon sand, but the sand is golden, and . . . it promises to be the greatest gold camp that has ever been known in the history of gold mining."[1]

In 1899 and 1900 the city upon the golden sands caught the imagination of men from all around the world. Though the creeks behind the city would produce far more gold in the long run than the beach, it was the easy diggings on the sandy shore that caused the rapid development of the city in 1899, and inspired most of the thousands who traveled to Nome in 1900.

Nome City, at the mouth of the Snake River, began as the campsite of the first prospectors who arrived in the area in the fall and early winter of 1898. By most of the laws of nature, Nome should have never been the site for a port city. There was no safe harbor for ships at the mouth of the Snake River, and it was dangerous to land or to take a small boat inside the mouth of the river. Large ships would be forced to anchor several miles offshore and unload their passengers and freight to lighters and shallow-draft barges that could be run up on the beach. In the years to come many men would drown for the lack of a safe harbor at Nome, and because of its exposed location every storm that swept across Norton Sound lashed the city as if it were a sinking ship. However, that mattered little to the men who were looking for gold in 1898. Because the site of Nome was so close to the rich claims on Anvil Creek and the other tributaries of the Snake River, it seemed at the time like a good location for a townsite.

In February 1899, a group of 42 men who had staked property and mining claims on the Snake River near Nome City, officially agreed to change the name of the new mining camp to Anvil City, because of the confusion with Nome River, which was located 4 miles to the southeast, and with Cape Nome, the point of land located 12 miles from the city.[2]

The name change only made the situation even more confusing. The town was locally known as Anvil City for much of 1899, but the United States Post Office Department insisted on calling the community "Nome," apparently because it was thought that a town called Anvil City would be easily confused with the village of Anvik on the lower Yukon. A competing townsite had been established at the mouth of the Nome River, and it was also called Nome City. The Anvil City merchants feared that the post office might decide to move the "Nome" post office from Anvil City on the Snake River to Nome City on the Nome River. After a vote was held the merchants reluctantly agreed to change the name of Anvil City back to Nome.[3]

Against its wishes the city was stuck with the unusual name of Nome. Unlike other towns which are proudly named for explorers, heroes, or politicians, the name of Nome came from a 50-year-old spelling mistake. In the 1850s an officer on a British ship off the coast of Alaska noted on a manuscript map that a nearby prominent point was not identified. He wrote "? Name" next to the point. When the map was recopied another draftsman thought that the ? was a C and that the a in "Name" was an o, and thus a mapmaker in the British Admiralty christened "Cape Nome."

In Nome itself, however, that theory was not widely known or generally accepted. The local belief was that the word Nome was derived from the Eskimo phrase

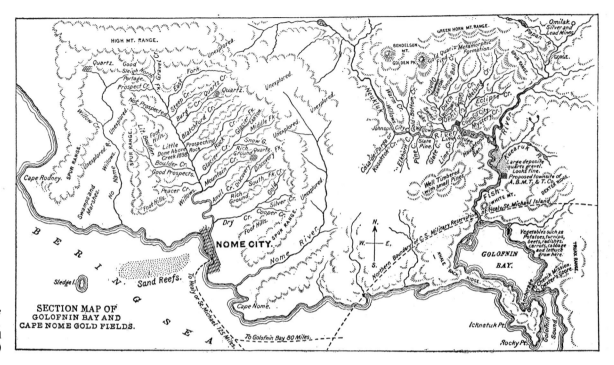

Kn-no-me, meaning "I don't know," and was probably an Eskimo reply when asked the name of the area.[5]

The city with the strange-sounding name at the mouth of the Snake River, which some early stampeders thought was spelled "Gnome," grew rapidly during 1899. A townsite covering 40 acres on both sides of the mouth of the Snake River was staked in the spring of 1899, and on March 24, a miners' meeting drew up a set of townsite laws. For a fee of $2.50 each man in the camp could stake and take possession of one town lot, provided that he started to make improvements on the property within 40 days. The miners ruled that $1.00 of each staking fee would be put into a fund for the construction of a hospital. The miners at the meeting envisioned the creation of a handsome city with blocks 300 feet square, and broad streets 60 feet wide. They also reserved one block for a public square.[6]

The lots in Nome were divided on a first-come, first-served basis. "At noon on April 4, 1899," the *Nome Nugget* later explained, "a shot was fired, and then began the scramble for lots.'"[7] Those who staked lots, however, were not always able to keep them. Lot jumping in the Nome district was as prevalent as claim jumping and it was not easy to get the materials to put up a shack or a cabin. There was not a decent-sized tree within one hundred miles of the townsite. Many of the prospectors built cabins with logs they had scavenged from the huge piles of driftwood on the beach, but most of them lived in white canvas tents.[8]

The young mining town already had need of a cemetery. A miners' meeting was held in early March to determine the cause of death of Ezra Carr, who had gotten lost in a storm and had been found dead on the tundra just outside the city of Nome. The meeting

After gold was discovered on the beach, hucksters and shopkeepers wasted no time in getting some of it for themselves. (Lulu Fairbanks Collection, University of Alaska Archives)

Partners working a poor man's surf rocker on the Nome beach. The men shoveled the sand on the washboard, and the waves washed out the gold.
(Ethel Becker)

but they could sing some of the songs of Zion and they did."[10]

It was no small matter to build a city on the banks of the Snake River, with all the amenities of civilization. When the first vessel with passengers bound for the Nome gold fields arrived in the roadstead on June 20, 1899, they found a "desolate forbidding spot," with a few driftwood log cabins and numerous tents. The area east of the Snake River, which later became the center of downtown Nome, consisted of one log cabin and three tents. The largest tent was a saloon.[11]

At first most of the people in the Nome district could hardly believe that this unusual community was built on a beach of golden sand. It seemed preposterous that gold could be found so easily. But when the destitutes at Nome realized that the beach was rich with gold, many of them must have thought they had died and gone to heaven. As one writer put it, after the beach strike Nome was a veritable "poor man's paradise — a land where no man has any excuse for being poor."[12] It was said that digging the gold out of the sand was easier than stealing it, and though the streets of Nome may have been covered with mud two feet deep, the beach was paved with gold.

The beach gold was mostly found in the ruby-colored sand, anywhere from one foot to four feet or more below the surface, but the richness of the sand varied greatly from place to place. The beach sands were not frozen, and therefore did not have to be thawed as the stream gravels did. The shallow diggings on the beach were open to everyone, and could not be located or staked by any one individual.[13] The general practice was that a miner was entitled to hold his space on the beach, sometimes the length of a shovel handle, as long as he worked it.

For good reason the men on the shore were often called beachcombers instead of miners.[14] The only equipment a man needed to work the golden sands was a shovel, a bucket or a large tin can with a handle to carry water, and a crude wooden rocker, also called a cradle, which

appointed a coroner's jury of 12 men which ruled, "that the said Ezra Carr became exhausted, fell upon his face in the snow and froze to death and this is our verdict." In 1902 the *Nome Nugget* proudly pointed out that Carr, the first man to die in Nome, had not been murdered. "Very frequently in the history of frontier towns," the *Nugget* explained, "the [first] funeral has been furnished with the aid of a gun. This was not the case, however, in the history of Nome."[9]

Not long after Carr's death, a French Canadian died from scurvy. Both men were buried at the same time, on a clear, cold day in March 1899. One witness said the services were as sad as anything he had ever seen. The camp did not have a clergyman, but all the miners in the district gathered to sing a few hymns. "There were no prayers said," one account of the event stated, "perhaps because the boys had forgotten those they used to say; at any rate all were out of practice in the praying line, pioneer miners had used throughout the West. The rocker was only one step beyond the gold pan in mining technology, and could be built by just about anyone handy with a hammer and saw.[15] To operate a rocker efficiently two or more men were needed. One man filled up the hopper on top of the cradle with the gold-bearing ruby sand, and while another poured a bucket of water over the sand, a third rocked the cradle vigorously back and forth. The lighter sand washed down through the hopper and out the bottom of the cradle, while the heavier flakes of gold would be caught on a blanket or a canvas screen, or else stopped by the wooden riffles in the bottom of the rocker. Finer gold was trapped by a copper plate in the bottom of the cradle which was covered with mercury. The mercury would form an amalgam with the gold and prevent it from being washed away.[16]

Though it had long been known that there were traces of gold in the sand along the beaches of the Seward Peninsula, it was not until July 1899 at Nome that prospectors realized that the sand was so rich. "The name of the man who first washed gold from this coast will in all probability never be known," the *Nome News* admitted in November 1899; however, it was generally agreed that the discovery was most likely made by several different people at the same time. As was fitting, it was probably one of the destitute miners stranded on the beach who "accidently discovered gold in the sand at his feet."[17]

A more puzzling mystery than the identity of the first discoverer of gold on the beach was the source of the gold. Almost everyone in Nome had their own favorite theory about the origin of the golden sands. Glaciers, volcanoes, meteors, or other "aberrations of nature" were among the most popular explanations. Charles D. Lane, a multimillionaire miner with nearly 50 years experience of mining in California, Idaho, Nevada, Arizona, and Alaska, had his own special theory. Lane was probably the wealthiest investor and capitalist in Nome's early years, and he did not believe, as some did, that the beach gold came from a glacier which had eroded a quartz ledge hidden somewhere in the mountains. He subscribed to the volcano theory. As Lane once explained,

> My reading of the books of nature tells me that the beach gold's source is not some hidden quartz ledge. I think it is the product of pent-up forces, through volcanic eruption, possibly, in the earth. It came from deep down in the bowels of the earth. These forces eventually belched forth the gold, which was probably washed back on the beach a short distance by the tides. I know my theory is at variance with that of the scientific men. I am a rough-and-tumble miner. I dig the gold from the ground where I find it, having no time for theories. If I fail to find it I move on.[18]

Another theory was that the gold fell from the sky. Peter L. Trout, who mined on the Nome beach in 1899, cited his experiences there as evidence for his general theory that the source of all the gold in the world was a "star mist" from outer space. Trout explained that "millions of fine particles" of gold had fallen from the skies in meteor showers and had washed up on the shore.[19]

Many weird machines were built to mine the golden sands. This contraption worked like an organ grinder. (Ethel Becker)

33

THE BEACH

*N*o thoughtful man who walked along this golden street in the bright sunlight of last October," one man wrote in 1900, "will ever forget the picture presented there." Working almost shoulder to shoulder with the simplest hand tools, the beach miners took small fortunes out of the golden sand. Some miners (left) used a rocker, while others (below) shoveled sand and water into a long tom. **Right** — Tents and mining machinery on the Nome beach in 1900 stretched away in the distance as far as the eye could see.

National Maritime Museum

A more common belief was that the gold on the beach had somehow precipitated out of the sea water, and that the golden sands extended for hundreds of miles along the Alaska coast, perhaps even as far north as Point Barrow.[20] Many men believed that the entire bottom of the Bering Sea was covered with gold, and that "the gold in the beach was inexhaustible because the supply was constantly renewed by the waves from the ocean bottom."[21] As one mining engineer explained it, "The prevailing belief is that chemical agency in sea-precipitation is responsible for the golden deposits, but quite a popular way of accounting for the thing is by regarding the sea bottom as a great vault which yields its golden sands to each successive storm in such a way as to replenish the wasted diggings that the miner leaves behind him."[22]

The miners at Nome who believed that the gold came in with the tide were right in the sense that the waves did form the beach placers. But the gold in the beach had actually been carried outward from the coastal plain by wave erosion, and concentrated on the beach, rather than tossed up from the bottom of a golden sea. Geologists

Alfred H. Brooks and F.C. Schrader visited the Nome beach in the fall of 1899, and their trained eyes saw that the gold on the beach had not come from the ocean, but had been washed out of the tundra. The geologists explained:

> The waves are constantly cutting away the base of the bluff that nearly everywhere bounds the tundra on the seaward side. As the material is thus eaten away the gravels and sands are carried seaward by the undertow, while the gold, because of its greater weight, is left on the beach. It works its way downward, more or less, in the loose sands near the water line, and may subsequently become buried.[23]

And though most everyone at Nome believed that the beach placers were unique, the geologists pointed out that similar, though less rich, beach deposits had been found in California, Oregon, New Zealand, and also in other parts of Alaska, including Yakutat Bay, Cook Inlet, and on the shores of Kodiak Island.[24]

Most of the beach miners however chose not to believe the explanations of the scientists, and liked their own theories better. In 1900 several thousand miners spent millions of dollars on dredging equipment and huge mechanical monsters to mine the bottom of the golden sea, only to find that the geologists were right, and that the sea bottom was not covered with gold. But no matter what the source of the gold, all could agree that the Nome beach in 1899 was one of the strangest sights any of them had ever seen.

"No thoughtful man who walked along this golden street in the bright sunlight of last October," wrote poet and census agent Sam Dunham in 1900, "will ever forget the picture presented there. For many miles along the beach double ranks of men were rocking, almost shoulder to shoulder, while their partners stripped the pay streak and supplied the rockers with water and pay dirt."[25]

At the height of the summer mining season, nearly two thousand men, women, and children were rocking on the

Miners battled the surf as they dug gold out of the beach sands. (Carrie McLain Museum)

These men hoped to get rich on the Nome beach by using a hand-cranked conveyor belt to mine the golden sands. (Ethel Becker)

beach, and it was estimated that they mined somewhere between $1 million and $2 million in gold from the sand. Many men averaged from $20 to $100 a day on the beach, and it was not unusual for a beach miner to have earned from $2,000 to $5,000 for his summer's labor. There were even reports that some of the luckiest men had rocked as much as $10,000 or $20,000 apiece from the golden sand.[26]

By the fall of 1899 Nome was a booming city of about five thousand people, thriving on the steady supply of gold that miners were rocking out of the beach sands. There were more saloons in the city than anything else, with at least 20 different drinking establishments in the community. The legal profession was a close second, with 16 lawyers operating in Nome by the end of the year. A wide variety of other shops had opened in Nome too, including:

1	brewery	2	meat markets
4	wholesale liquor stores	1	boot and shoe store
1	massage artiste	1	book and stationery store
6	bakers	3	packers and forwarders
5	laundries		
12	general merchandise stores	2	dentists
		11	physicians
3	second hand stores	1	mining engineer
4	hotels	2	surveyors
6	restaurants	4	bath houses
6	lodging-houses	1	bank and safe deposit
4	real estate offices	2	printing offices
2	paper-hangers	1	confectionery store
3	fruit and cigar stores	1	blacksmith shop
		1	assay office
2	tinshops	2	contractors and builders
4	drugstores		
2	photographers	2	hospitals
3	watchmakers	4	barber shops
2	sign-painters	2	clubs[27]

In September 1899, United States census agent Arthur F. Wines counted about five hundred tents which were pitched in the Nome area, and at least two hundred wood-frame buildings, either finished or under construction. "An absolutely accurate count could hardly be made," Wines explained, "on account of the irregular way in which tents and buildings are located."[28]

The lots were not uniformly laid out, and lot jumping went on constantly. Cabins and large buildings were often built in the middle of what were supposed to be streets. The center of the Nome business district on Front Street was actually located outside of the original townsite that the pioneers of the camp had staked on paper in the spring of 1899. The bitter competition for choice business lots and the lack of an adequate plat of the city were two reasons why the streets of gold rush Nome were so narrow. Some of the city's streets were only eight feet wide. In 1899, however, the streets of Nome were mostly imaginary anyway.

"There were streets on the map of Nome," an early history of Nome states, "but the observer could not distinguish them in the town."[29] The winding trails through the hundreds of cabins and tents in the city were rivers of mud, two feet deep, and gum boots were an absolute necessity to get around town. It was said that a pedestrian walking along Front Street in 1899 "was at times uncertain whether he would arrive at his destination or suddenly find himself in China."[30]

Besides almost impassable streets, sanitation was another serious problem in the soggy townsite. Doctors feared an epidemic as sewage and garbage were commonly dumped into the Snake River, which at that time was the source of much of the community's drinking water. There were few public "closets" in Nome, and typhoid fever, bloody dysentery, and pneumonia were all common. Dysentery was especially severe among newcomers and hard drinkers. A physician reported that "one would see blood in every public convenience." The townsite was poorly drained, and living conditions were

Though prices were high, Nome's grocery stores had a wide selection of goods, from Iron Beer to Mother's Bread.
(Bancroft Library)

A Retail Store, Nome, Alaska.

RESTAURANT

STEAMSHIP OFFICE.

L. COHEN

CIGARS

FRONT STREET NOME

397-D

rugged. "Most of the people are living in crowded tents, which are seldom in a cleanly condition," census agent Wines commented, and it appeared that unless some action was taken, the consequences would be disastrous.[31]

To establish order in the city, Alaska District Judge Charles Johnson, who visited Nome in August 1899, urged the city leaders to organize a "consent government," that could enforce health regulations, pass local laws, and provide the services that a city of several thousand people would need to survive the winter. The people of Nome had no legal right to create a municipal government, because Congress had not passed legislation permitting the establishment of local governments in Alaska. But Washington, D.C., was far away, and with the consent of most of the people in Nome, a miners' meeting decided to form a local government. An election for a mayor, city council, chief of police, and other city officials was held on September 12, 1899. About fourteen hundred votes were cast in the election. Some of the civic-minded Nomeites voted not once but several times for their favorite candidates, as "voters were not registered and repeating was easy."[32] The election was also remarkable because the few women in Nome were permitted to vote, long before women's suffrage was accepted nationwide. The "miner's ticket" swept the election, with Thomas D. Cashel chosen as the first mayor of the city of Nome's consent government.

Cashel appointed Key Pittman, a 27-year-old lawyer who had come down the Yukon from Dawson City earlier in the year, to be the first city attorney of Nome. Pittman was an able lawyer and a gifted politician. Later in his career he was elected six times to the United States Senate by the people of the state of Nevada, and he rose to become the chairman of the Senate Foreign Relations Committee in the 1930s. His first political job was his appointment as Nome's city attorney in 1899, at a salary of $2,400 a year, a salary which was second only on the city payroll to Mayor Cashel's $2,500 a year.

Mayor Cashel needed a clever city attorney because the consent government had no legal authority to enforce its regulations, or to make Nome residents pay the city's local taxes, and had to rely on voluntary compliance with the law. As the winter months passed fewer and fewer volunteer taxpayers were to be found. By the spring of 1900, with the combination of a large city payroll and a shrinking number of taxpayers, the consent government ran out of money.[33] Also by that time the sanitation problem in Nome was more severe than it had been earlier. Mayor Cashel said in late February, "The alleyways between some of the prominent saloons on Front Street are almost three feet deep with a glacier of urine." The main streets were just as bad. "Our thoroughfares are almost impassable for vehicles," Cashel said, "and dangerous to pedestrians."[34]

Yet the consent government did provide some important services for the city of Nome during its first year of existence, before it ran completely out of money. The fire department kept the city from burning down in the winter of 1899-1900, and the police department maintained order. Only five people died "violent deaths" during Nome's first winter, and only one man was murdered.[35] Some of the questionable characters in Nome had been deported or blue-ticketed in the fall of 1899 by the city government and given a free ride south on a United States revenue cutter, as were numerous destitute men who did not have the price of a ticket, and had no means of supporting themselves for the winter.

But many of the people of Nome in the fall of 1899 had no desire to remain for the winter. The fear of running out of food during the long winter months, the real threat of a typhoid epidemic, and the scarcity of adequate shelter convinced many that they should spend the winter in a milder climate. Most of them could tell spectacular stories of the riches at Nome, and they had bags of gold dust to prove it. While the people left at the new city of Nome struggled to survive their first winter, the news of the golden beaches on the Bering Sea spread across the United States.

In February 1900 the alleyways between the saloons on Front Street were "almost three feet deep with a glacier of urine." (Ethel Becker)

Chapter III
The City on the Golden Sand

At first few people outside of Nome believed the rumors that the miners on the Nome beach had discovered gold in the sand. It seemed impossible. But when the last ships from the new gold camp reached Seattle in the fall of 1899, they were fully loaded with men from Nome who had "thousands upon thousands of dollars in dust and nuggets."[1] The total gold production on the Nome beach in 1899 was probably between $1 million and $2 million, while a few dozen creek claims that were being developed were also turning out to be fabulously rich, producing nearly $1.5 million in gold.[2]

Slowly the doubters began to take the story of the Nome strike seriously.

The first community to feel the effect of the discovery of gold in the Nome beach sand was Dawson City, where reports of the strike had begun to arrive in the late summer of 1899. By fall a stampede was under way. Nearly fifteen hundred people left Dawson for Nome on the last sternwheelers going down the Yukon in 1899. Hundreds of others waited until the Yukon froze over, and then mushed their dogs down the river ice to the new gold fields. The exodus to the new camp continued all winter long, and threatened to depopulate Dawson City.

"The gold fever is no respector of persons," a Dawson City newspaper warned its readers. "Like the dew of heaven it falls with absolute impartiality upon the just and the unjust alike. Its germs once planted in the system, take root and thrive so vigorously that it dominates its victim like an all consuming passion for drink."[3]

Some of the "Nomads" had dog teams or horse-drawn sleds. Others went the poor man's route and walked all the way with ropes over their shoulders pulling small hand sleds behind them. One big Norwegian with Nome fever skated down the Yukon River, averaging about 40 miles a day in places where the ice was smooth. Most unusual of all, however, were those "Nomers" who rode their bicycles to the new gold fields.

The bicycle craze of the 1890s was still going strong during the Alaska gold rush, and many gold seekers made long-distance bicycle trips through the wilderness, exploits that would seem impossible today. One of these intrepid wheelmen was Edward Jesson, a young miner in Dawson City who caught the Nome fever in February 1900. He decided that a $150 "wheel" that he had seen for sale in Dawson City might be the best way to get to Nome, and so he bought it. Jesson described his brother's reaction to his plan.

> What the hell are you going to do with the wheel he asked. Going to Nome, I said. He called Harry Smith and John Nelson proprietors of the hotel and some other oldtimers. He said this brother of mine is going to try to go to Nome on a bicycle. He's crazy, they all said. We will have him put on the wood-pile until he comes out of it.[4]

Jesson practiced on the bike in Dawson City for eight days, learning how to keep his wheel inside an 18-inch sled track without falling down, and then started pedaling to Nome.

He made excellent time on the trail, usually passing every dog team in sight, but found the weather was far from ideal for cycling. One morning in late February the

A traffic jam on Front Street in 1900. (Ethel Becker)

Ed Jesson was one of several wheelmen who went to Nome the hard way, on a bicycle. (Museum of History and Industry)

temperature dropped to 48° below zero. "The rubber tires on my wheel were frozen and I could scarcely ride it and my nose was freezing and I had to hold the handlebars with both hands not being able to ride yet with one hand and rub my nose with the other." At one spot on the river ice he fell and broke his handlebars, which he replaced with spruce boughs, and nearly broke his knee. He fell so often, however, that his body was covered with bruises, and everyone he met thought he was crazy. The Indians along the Yukon River, most of whom had never seen a bicycle before, were greatly amused by Jesson's wheel. "White man he sit down walk like hell," one of them said.

Jesson was pleased with the way that his bicycle held up on the trip, and he did not break a spoke or puncture a tire for the whole way. He thought his bicycle was not only faster than most dog teams, but was also better equipped to navigate the roughest parts of the trail. Near Tanana on the Yukon River many of the horses and dogs had cut their feet. "The trail was bloody for miles from the bleeding and limping dogs," Jesson wrote. While

many of the mushers had sprained their ankles there, he was able to cruise right by them on his bicycle.[5]

Ed Jesson wheeled his silent steed onto the streets of Nome on the afternoon of March 29, 1900, after riding more than one thousand miles across Alaska in five weeks. His bicycle was in better shape than he was. Jesson was nearly snowblind by the time he reached Nome and his eyes were so sore he did not recognize the face of an old friend who met him on the street.

The town into which Ed Jesson rode in March 1900 was one of the most isolated communities in the world. The city of about three thousand people had been cut off from direct contact with the outside world for almost half a year, and it was hungry for news.

"Four months have nearly passed since we have had any communication with the outside world," the *Nome News* had stated on December 30, 1899. At that time the editor of the paper, J.F.A. Strong, had wondered what had happened in the rest of the country since the last outside newspapers, dated October 9, 1899, had reached Nome. "We cannot help but be curious, even anxious, to know something about outside affairs," Strong confessed. "Especially are we concerned as to the affairs of our government and people." Strong took it "for granted" that McKinley would be renominated by the Republicans, but who would replace Bryan on the Democratic ticket? Had the Philippine war been settled, or was it still going on? And what about "the outcome of the threatened war between Great Britain and the Transvaal?" Strong said that some of these issues had probably already been "settled and forgotten ere this, but to us, who are in banishment for a season, they are as yet burning and vital questions."[6]

Three months later when lone wheelman Ed Jesson pedaled into Nome, he brought some of the answers. Jesson carried with him from Dawson City several outside newspapers, including copies of the *Seattle Post-Intelligencer* and the *San Francisco Examiner*, which announced that the United States had won the war against the rebels in the Philippines. Though the news was actually premature, it gave the isolated community of Nome an occasion to celebrate all night long. Volunteers stood up at a dance hall and took turns reading from the columns of the *Post-Intelligencer* and the *Examiner,* while others proposed toasts to the battleship *Oregon,* Admiral Dewey, and anyone or anything else they could think of.[7]

The most important news for the people of Nome, however, were the reports in the *Seattle Post-Intelligencer* of the thousands of men who were gathering at Seattle, and preparing to come to Nome as soon as the ice was gone from the Bering Sea.[8] Within the next six to eight weeks it was estimated that a massive invasion of perhaps 50,000 to 100,000 gold seekers would leave the west coast of Canada and the United States for the city on the golden sand. There was no way on earth that the town could have been prepared for what was to happen.

It was believed that once the ice was gone from the Bering Sea, the rush of gold seekers to Nome might be even larger than the stampede to the Klondike had been two years earlier, because it was so much easier to get to Nome. The Klondikers in 1898 had been forced to climb the Chilkoot Pass, carrying enough supplies on their backs to last them a year, and build boats at the headwaters of the Yukon to float hundreds of miles down the treacherous river all the way to Dawson City. In comparison a trip to Nome was a holiday cruise. "It is child's play to reach it," a guidebook for the Nome stampeders stated, "and none of the hardships of the first journey to the Klondike will be experienced."[9] Those who went to Nome in 1900 did not have to climb mountains, run river rapids, or even pack their own supplies. A Nomer could leave his home in London, New York, or San Francisco, and travel all the way to the Nome gold fields by modern passenger train and steamship.

Nome was one of the most inaccessible places in the world during the winter when the Bering Sea was covered with ice, but the city was easily reached by boat between

the months of June and October. The most dangerous part of the entire voyage was probably getting off the ship in Nome. Because there was no harbor, all the big ships had to anchor in the Nome roadstead a mile or more off the coast, and all freight and passengers had to be lightered ashore.[10] The major part of the journey, however, was comparatively safe and easy. Instead of sleeping in tents along the trail, and living off of flour and beans, Nome pioneers camped out in bunk beds and staterooms, and ate their meals at dining room tables.

Though it could be easily reached by steamship in the summer, Nome was one of the most inaccessible cities in the world during the winter. (Bancroft Library)

45

Nome Gold

Poor Man's Diggings
American Soil
8 Days from Seattle

ROCKING AND SLUICING BEACH SAND AT NOME, SEPTEMBER, 1899

VIA

N.A.T.&T.CO.

PROPERTY OF UNIV. OF ALASKA LIB.

NORTH AMERICAN
TRANSPORTATION AND
TRADING CO.'S ROUTE

The Quickest Service ❧ ❧ Cheapest in Price

For Reservations of Berths and Freight Space, address

North American Transportation & Trading Co.

CHICAGO, ILLINOIS   SEATTLE, WASHINGTON

It sounded so easy and so inexpensive too. The cost of a second-class ticket from Seattle to Nome was only $60 or $70. At that price there were few dreamers and fortune hunters who could resist the appeals that the railroad and steamship companies published all across the country. One advertisement stated:

WOULD YOU LIKE TO BE A MILLIONAIRE?

Few men become rich by slow economy. Fortunes are made by men of nerve and decision who take advantage of opportunities. CAPE NOME, Alaska, offers YOU the chance of your whole life. Hundreds of men will dig out a fortune next year. Why not you? Cape Nome is easily reached. No walking or packing. Steamers run DIRECT from SEATTLE to NOME CITY. The GREAT NORTHERN RAILWAY will take you to Seattle in two-and-one-half days, from St. Paul. Direct steamer connections.[11]

By May 1900, the streets of the city of Seattle were choked with Nome stampeders, as "Nome Fever" overwhelmed the city. The population of Seattle was about 80,000, but it was believed that there may have been an additional 20,000 people in the city because of the Nome stampede. In the crowded shops and stores on Second Avenue the Nome stampeders could buy men's and women's Nome underwear (guaranteed to be both wind- and frost-proof), Nome gasoline stoves, Nome scurvy cures, Nome water filters, Nome tents, Nome medicines to put in their Nome medicine chests, and many other invaluable products.

The most ingenious Nome inventions were the contraptions designed to mine gold from the beach sands. According to one count, at least 35 different kinds of patent gold saving devices and gold washing machines were on sale in Seattle, each guaranteed to be the only practical method for mining out millions on the Nome beach. Some of the machines were relatively modest, like Swain's Improved Gold Amalgamator, which could handle up to a ton of beach sand per hour; Yoho's Scien-

The transportation companies promised that a trip to Nome would be as easy as child's play. (University of Alaska Archives)

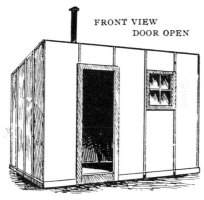
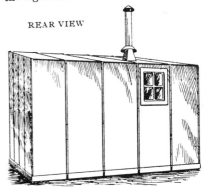

University of Washington Library

NOME FEVER

NOME was a magic word in the spring of 1900. Tens of thousands of people dreamed of riches in the golden sands of the Bering Sea, and advertisers in Seattle were quick to cash in on Nome Fever. Anyone with anything to sell, from a medicine chest to a cash register, claimed that their product was the only brand for Nome.

University of Washington Library

University of Washington Library

tific Gold Trap, which was designed along "scientific principles" but could be "operated by a boy;" and Reeve's Cape Nome Rocker, which only weighed 40 pounds and cost $15.[12] Other machines were more complicated and had as many cogs, whistles, screens, valves, and tubes on them as possible. A popular claim of one of the more unlikely looking Cape Nome gold extractors was stated by a young cigar-smoking salesman on a Seattle street corner: "What we claims fer this machine, gentlemen, is that it gives the genuine motion of the gold pan in the hands of an old time prospector."[13]

The first ships to leave for Nome, filled with both greenhorns and genuine old-time prospectors, left Seattle in mid-April, but the largest part of the Nome fleet did not depart until May or June. This great seagoing armada of 50 or 60 vessels included dozens of two- and three-masted sailing ships, barges and tugboats, small steamers, and ocean liners. The biggest ships were the huge passenger liners, each one loaded like the Ark. The *Centennial* had 639 passengers on board and 80 head of livestock. The *Ohio* carried 706 people, and 1,500 tons of freight. The *Senator* had 499 people on her passenger list. There were 604 on the *Oregon*, 575 on the *Roanoke*, about 500 on the *Victoria*, and close to 400 on the *Santa Ana*.[58] According to one estimate, the 30 steamers that left Seattle for Nome in May and June carried a total of about 11,000 passengers.[14]

On one day alone, May 20, four ships left Seattle carrying 5,000 tons of mining machinery and other supplies and about 1,200 people to Nome. It was estimated that 12,000 people came to see them off. The crowds were so heavy that there was an "extensive paralysis" on the city's streets, with large traffic jams along the waterfront, and delays of many hours for the ships. Among the freight shipped that day to Nome was a $10,000 load of "bar fixtures, buggies and general merchandise," a newspaper and job printing plant, a "complete banking outfit, including $200,000 in coin and currency" for the newly established Bank of Cape Nome,

a "thirty ton outfit of liquors and bar fixtures" for a new saloon, the rails and most of the equipment for a seven-mile-long narrow-gauge railroad, 300,000 feet of lumber, 600 tons of coal, and many more tons of general merchandise and mining equipment.[15]

The ships that headed north carried knocked-down theaters, gambling halls, saloons, hotels, restaurants, and everything else needed to construct an instant civilization on the shores of the Bering Sea, including more than eight million feet of lumber.[16] "This will be the strangest community ever seen upon the face of this old earth," the *Seattle Post-Intelligencer* predicted, "for it will combine the extremes of primitive rudeness and high civilization."[17] Nome promised to be as much an "Arctic Coney Island" as a traditional mining camp.

The Nome fleet headed straight across the North Pacific, and the ships were usually out of sight of land

Above — *One of many companies which was looking for backers to finance an expedition to Nome.* **Right** — *Crowds along the Seattle waterfront as the SS* Ohio *prepares to depart for Nome in May 1900.*
(Both photos University of Washington Library)

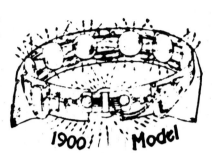
for a week or 10 days until they arrived in the Aleutian Islands. Conditions on most of the vessels were far from comfortable. Every ship was badly overcrowded, and all accounts agree that the food was terrible. Many of the Nomers had never been at sea before, and more than a few were seasick for most of the trip. They often swore they would never take another ocean voyage again, and some men feared they might have to live in Nome forever. No one enjoyed listening to dozens of other passengers coughing, heaving, and throwing up all day, especially when one's own stomach felt uneasy.

One of the Nome passengers who was worried about seasickness was 19-year-old Carl Lomen from Minnesota, who was traveling to Nome on a vacation with his father Gudbrand J. Lomen. The Lomen family eventually became famous for their extensive holdings in reindeer, which they attempted to develop into an industry like sheepherding or cattle ranching, and a variety of other businesses in northwestern Alaska, including shipping, lightering, photography, and general merchandising. In 1900, however, the future "Reindeer King" had more immediate concerns. The Lomens had two first-class berths on the *Garonne,* which departed Seattle on May 23. One day out of port Carl Lomen wrote in his small leather-bound diary, "Have been real anxious the last few days to get to sea so as to find out whether I would be sea-sick or not. Plead guilty. Feeling very funny now." A day later he felt even worse. "Got em bad," he scribbled in his diary on May 25. "Don't even agree with me to look at anything to eat. Take an orange or cracker. Stay on deck the whole day."[18]

After a few days most of the passengers found their sea legs, and they tried to amuse themselves as best they could. After all the excitement at leaving port, the routine at sea was boring. "Life on ship board is about the same day after day," one restless fortune hunter wrote to his wife six days north of Seattle. "Eat, sit, walk, eat, sit, walk, eat, sleep, with a little conversation, lots of gossip, some cards, etc. thrown in. And after noon each day see

Left — Dr. Sanden's Electric Belt was guaranteed to protect "Cape Nomers" from a wide assortment of ailments. Right — A traffic jam on the Seattle waterfront, with a ship about to leave for Nome. (Both photos University of Washington Library)

how many miles we have run in the past twenty-four hours."[19]

Most of the ships destined for Nome stopped at least briefly at Unalaska, the village near Dutch Harbor. The ships' captains took on coal or water there, or waited for a clear channel through the ice pack. North of Dutch Harbor, the Nome gold seekers had their first experience with ice navigation. The grinding of the ice pack was a sound that novices did not soon forget. As one Nome passenger wrote, after his ship had safely wound its way through 250 miles of ice to Nome, "It was a toss up many a time whether we were going through the ice or whether the ice was going through us."[20]

By early June the ice in the Bering Sea was still quite solid, but a voyage through the shifting ice pack was necessary, otherwise a vessel might not arrive at Nome until the middle of the summer. Every ship wanted to be the first to get to Nome; the gold seekers were as enthusiastic as the fans at a college football game, and they cheered or booed as they passed, or were passed, by a rival vessel. But this race was not to the swift alone. Navigating through the ice was a risky business, and solid masses of ice could force steamships to travel hundreds of miles out of their way looking for a channel to get beyond them. Ships could be tossed around like toys by the movement of the ice. James Galen, the son-in-law of Sen. Thomas H. Carter of Montana, was a passenger on board the *Tacoma*. On June 10 he described the race through the ice pack in a letter he wrote to his sisters in Montana.

> Well we didn't get to Nome today and it is hard to tell when we will. Ice all around us. This morning we sighted the *Ohio* which left Seattle on May 26th and the *Chas Nelson* which sailed from same port on May 19th. . . . We have seen nothing but fields of ice all day but we have been winding around until we are about thirty miles nearer Nome than we were this morning. Just passed the *Aberdeen* which left Seattle May 19th. She says she met the *Olympian* going back to Dutch Harbor on account of the ice. She gave us the information that there is "too much ice ahead." Our Captain called back "not too much for me" and all the *Tacoma* passengers cheered.[21]

The passengers on the *Tacoma* were not cheering about four hours later, when the ship was trapped by a large iceberg and forced hard aground in seven feet of mud. Galen feared that the *Tacoma* would be stuck for a month, or at least until all of the other vessels had unloaded their cargo at Nome. The *Aberdeen,* the ship which Galen and his fellow passengers had given "the laugh" a few hours earlier, refused to help as that might mean they would be delayed in arriving at Nome. "The only place you can find sympathy between these tramp steamers," Galen wrote, "is in the dictionary under 'S.' "[22] After being stuck in the mud for three days, the *Tacoma* eventually worked its way free by throwing 350 tons of coal overboard to lighten her draft, and she continued through the grinding ice pack.

The first ship of the fleet to arrive at Nome was the steam whaler *Alexander,* which anchored in the roadstead on May 21. The first person to come ashore was Dan Sutherland, who was to become Alaska's delegate in the United States Congress in the 1920s.[23] The first passenger vessel to reach Nome was the steam schooner *Jeanie* of the Pacific Steam Whaling Company, which arrived 48 hours later.[24] In the weeks to come more than 50 steamships and between 15,000 and 20,000 people followed her through the ice to one of the most unique cities in the entire world. "It was a sight," one early writer said of Nome, "to be seen but once in a lifetime."[25]

Passengers stare ahead anxiously as their ship navigates through the ice pack. (Leta Hamilton)

Tents, lumber, and other supplies are spread out along the Nome beach in 1900, as well as several large dredges under construction on the water's edge. (University of Alaska Archives, reprinted from The ALASKA JOURNAL®)

Chapter IV
On the Beach

During the summer of 1900, Nome was the busiest seaport in the world without a harbor. "A fleet larger than the British used in their war with South Africa rides at anchor in these northern waters," a Nome stampeder wrote in 1900. "A line of white tents longer than the water front of Seattle lay glittering in the midnight sun." Captain David H. Jarvis of the revenue cutter service estimated that by the end of the summer, perhaps as many as 18,000 people had landed at Nome, while about 10,000 had left. Probably about 15,000 gold seekers and about 600,000 tons of freight arrived during the month of June.[1] Every day dozens of ships unloaded hopeful arrivals and mountains of cargo while other vessels were filling up just as rapidly with those who were anxious to return home.

"Never again, in all human probability," the *Nome News* wrote on June 23, "will similar scenes be enacted as have marked the appearances of scores of vessels in the harbor and the ingress of thousands of people on the Bering Sea coast since the opening of navigation on May 21."[2] It was a scene, the newspaper thought, that was "worthy of the brush of an artist of renown." A fleet of ships was anchored under the midnight sun like the vessels of an invading army about to come ashore.

From the deck of a ship entering the Nome roadstead, the beach appeared to be covered with snow.[3] Only upon coming closer to the shore, did the new arrivals realize that the snowbanks were really thousands upon thousands of tents which gold seekers had staked for miles along the shoreline. Every ship announced its arrival with several whistle blasts, and each ship answered in return. Relieved to be finally out of the ice

pack, and in sight of the tent city on the beach for which they had come so far, the passengers cheered and applauded. Everyone was eager to get ashore as soon as possible, and more than one crew member deserted at the first opportunity.

The gold seekers, however, still faced the most hazardous part of the journey by sea to Nome, getting off the ship. Lightering the thousands of people and hundreds of thousands of tons of freight ashore on the Nome beach was a complex amphibious operation. It cost almost as much to carry a load of freight the last mile through the surf from the ship to the shore, as it had cost to transport it more than two thousand miles from Seattle. In rough weather or a high wind nothing could be loaded or unloaded, and even in calm seas few people got ashore without getting wet.

Passengers climbed into barges that were pulled to within about 30 feet of the shore, and then let drift through the breakers. "Women were carried ashore on the backs of men who waded out to the lighters," explained Lanier McKee, who landed at Nome in 1900, "and the men, for the most part, completed the remaining distance in their rubber boots, or got wet, or imposed upon the back and good nature of some accommodating person."[4]

As the gold seekers came ashore on the golden sands, the mining camp they saw was one of the strangest gold rush boom towns in the history of the American West.

The greenhorns who landed at Nome might have thought they were on another planet, and not just 2,300 miles north of Seattle, or 2,700 miles from San Francisco. They had come to a land where broad daylight lasted all

*A mountain of freight lined the Nome beach, and teamsters
charged exorbitant prices to haul it away.*
(Seppala Collection, University of Alaska Archives)

night long, but they knew that the sun would nearly disappear during the winter, when the weather turned so cold that the sea itself froze over. The landscape was barren of trees and called tundra, a new word to most of the gold seekers, and was usually shrouded with clouds of millions of mosquitoes.

After returning from Nome in 1900, Arthur L. Pearse, an English mining engineer, pictured the scene at Nome for his colleagues in a speech he gave at the Museum of Practical Geology in London. He described what he called "a most unique mining camp."

Imagine a heterogeneous mob of 23,000 people landed on a beach, mostly without any kind of shelter except what they brought with them; the majority knowing nothing of the kind of place they were coming to until they landed; many having left home for the first time; a few miners and storekeepers, some labourers who would be miners, many landsharks, lawyers, saloon-men, and speculators; men and women expecting to grow rich by magic out of the golden sands; huddled together on the strip of beach sixty feet wide, this being the only free land from high water to sixty feet above; without any sanitary arrangements; sleeping on almost frozen ground at night, broiling in a hot sun by day; and you have Nome as it was.[5]

On the beach there was total chaos. The first sight that greeted the gold seekers as they came ashore was the mountain of freight stacked on the sand. The longshoremen wearing hip boots or walking on planks from the barges to the beach carried tons of freight ashore and dumped it on the sand just beyond the water's edge.

It was almost impossible for anyone to locate his own freight or luggage in the confusion. Everything from pianos to sewing machines, bar fixtures and barrels of whiskey, was stacked along the beach, as well as huge shipments of lumber, grain, hay, general merchandise, mining machinery, hardware, and food. Many of the boxes and crates were smashed open. A $10,000 shipment of canned goods broke apart, and all the labels washed off the cans. The owners could not tell one can from another, so all of them had to be stacked in a huge pile and sold "as is" for 10¢ apiece.[6]

Charles Draper, a New York man who landed at Nome during the big stampede, wrote that the freight was stacked "so close to the water's edge that you had to watch your chance between waves to get past and avoid a wetting."[7] Draper said the beach was thronged with thousands of dogs, and altogether he thought it was "as crazy a scene as an adventurer ever witnessed."[8]

Coming ashore by barge at Nome. (Ethel Becker)

The scene got even crazier, however, along the narrow sandy path called Front Street, as the thousands of men and dogs jammed the center of the city. Draper wrote,

As for Nome itself, I found it about the oddest excuse for a town I ever ran across. The master mind that laid it out seemed to have but two things in view — to keep near enough to the edge of the tundra to occasionally find dry footing, and at the same time far enough from the actual sea level to be just beyond the reach of the waves when the sea should get boisterous. As a result the town site was little better than a line — all length and no breadth.[9]

The city of Nome was about two blocks wide and five miles long. Front Street was the main thoroughfare of the city, and in places it was less than 15 feet wide.[10] In the heart of the city where the biggest saloons, gambling houses, hotels, and restaurants were located, the crowds jammed the street from storefront to storefront. "The crowding and bustle there was something I had never seen before and never expect to see again," one man explained after he returned to Seattle. In the tiny street, he said, 25,000 people were "all rushing hither and thither like madmen, elbowing one another for room — a perfect Babel of noise."[11]

When the weather was dry, as it was throughout the early summer of 1900, Front Street was a dust bowl. When the rains came later in the summer the sandy roadway turned into a river of mud, and men and horses alike could nearly drown in the muck trying to cross from one side of the street to the other. For that reason the main streets were eventually paved with wooden planks three inches thick.

Because it was light all night long, there were often as many people on the streets of Nome at one o'clock in the morning as there were at one o'clock in the afternoon. Everywhere new buildings were under construction; besides the roar of the sea, the constant noise in the background was the sound of the hammer and the saw. "The

growth of Nome during the past thirty days has never been equaled at any point in the United States," the *Nome Gold Digger* boasted on July 4.

Stately business blocks spring up as if by magic, rich and costly interiors are finished in a night, and where an old unsightly shack stood forty-eight hours ago, a handsome structure, three stories in height, looms with storerooms filled with bright new goods, while the upper floors, divided into office suites, teem with professional life and activity. Such is Nome as she strides on toward the zenith of her glory when she will be the greatest mining camp city the world has ever known.[12]

Every nail and every board foot of lumber used in Nome had traveled two or three thousand miles by ship before being unloaded on the Nome beach; and almost everything in Nome cost from two to five times as much as it did in Seattle or San Francisco.[13] "The expenses of

Some of Nome's streets were less than eight feet wide. (Howard Hein)

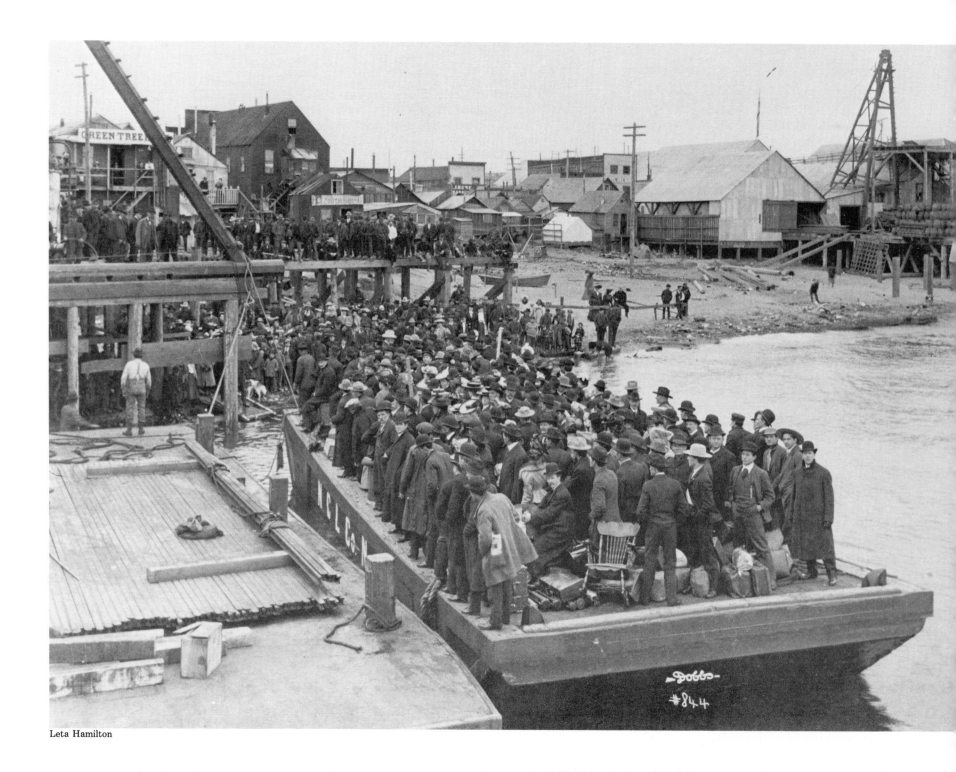

Leta Hamilton

GETTING ASHORE

*T*he hardest part of the journey to Nome was getting off the ship. Because Nome did not have a deep-water harbor, passengers had to be lightered ashore like an invading army. The lighters were pulled ashore as close as possible, and then the passengers got off as best they could. "Women were carried ashore on the backs of men who waded out to the lighters," one man wrote, "and the men, for the most part, completed the remaining distance in their rubber boots, or got wet, or imposed upon the back and good nature of some accommodating person."

The lighter on the left carries a full load of passengers, their baggage, and a rocking chair.
Right — *Another barge load coming ashore.*
Below — *Fighting breakers on the beach, longshoremen carry a load of lumber ashore piece by piece.*

Ethel Becker

Anchorage Historical and Fine Arts Museum

living in this place have reached a point beyond anything that I ever dreamt of,'' wrote C.S.A. Frost, an investigator whom the United States attorney general's office sent to Nome in the summer of 1900. He could not believe that common laborers in Nome were paid $1.00 an hour, carpenters received $1.50 an hour, and waiters made from $5.00 to $7.00 a day. "There is nothing with the possible exception of a box of matches and a two-cent postage stamp that sells for less than twenty-five cents," Frost explained.[14]

Office space in Nome was extremely expensive, when it was available at all. Lawyers and anyone else who hung out a shingle were usually "packed in their tiny offices like sardines in a box."[15] An 8-by-10-foot office, about the size of a big closet, Frost complained, without plaster on the walls, "without heat, light, or janitor service or furniture of any description rents readily for from forty to sixty dollars per month."[16]

The high cost of lumber and construction materials made it impossible for most of the gold seekers at Nome to build their own cabins or shacks. The few hotels in Nome were filled, and newly arriving gold seekers without their own tents had to sleep on the streets or the beach. Shelter was improvised with the use of boats turned on their sides, and abandoned packing crates. The sternwheelers which had brought passengers to Nome from Saint Michael were also used; the owners of several steam boats tied up their vessels inside the mouth of the Snake River, and transformed them into floating hospitals, hotels, boardinghouses, and restaurants, similar to the way the forty-niners had used their old sailing ships, once they had landed in San Francisco Bay.

The *Minneapolis* became a private hospital and boarding-house, while the steamers *Quickstep* and *City of Chicago* were remodeled into two of the leading hotels in the city.

T.J. Nestor's *City of Chicago* was reportedly the first hotel in Nome.[17] He docked and remodeled the boat and opened both a restaurant and a beer garden on board. The hotel could accommodate 175 guests, with spring beds costing 50¢ a night and private rooms for $1. If a man so chose, he could let the hours sail away in the *City of Chicago* bar, drinking 10-year-old whiskey and smoking Key West cigars.

For the many men, however, who could not afford to rent a room for the night, and had to sleep on the ground in blankets, the high point of their day was getting a letter from home. Like everything else in Nome the mail was backlogged. Since the community had more people without an address or a permanent home than any place in the country, the city of Nome in 1900 had the largest general delivery service in the United States.[18] Five filing boxes were needed just for the Johnsons alone. The line to pick up mail at the post office often wound around the block, and it was not uncommon for Nome residents to have to wait in line several hours to pick up a letter.

The inspector at the Nome post office was John Clum, the man who years earlier in Arizona had founded the *Tombstone Epitaph*, and was used to the problems of life in a new mining camp. In the 30-by-35-foot shack that served as the post office, Clum employed 24 clerks, working round the clock at sorting the mail in three eight-hour shifts. Every day the Seattle post office handled about a half-ton of mail addressed to people at Nome; by mid-July an average of four pounds of mail had been sent to every resident of Nome, and the backlog in the Nome post office was monumental.[19] It sometimes took months for letters to be delivered.

To ease the congestion at the post office, Clum hired two resourceful mail carriers who were on leave of absence from the post office in Portland, to deliver the mail to businesses with permanent addresses. Fred Lockley and Ben Taylor had taken two of their old

For one brief summer, Nome was one of the busiest seaports in the world. (National Maritime Museum)

Drinking up at the Arctic Cafe Saloon in Nome. (Lulu Fairbanks Collection, University of Alaska Archives)

buildings in town. Wyatt Earp's Dexter, Tex Rickard's Northern, Charles Cobb's Horseshoe, William Robertson's Eldorado, and others were all popular watering holes. One of the favorites was the Baldwin, run by E.J. ("Lucky") Baldwin of San Francisco.

Lucky Baldwin was an eccentric millionaire who had made his fortune in the Comstock Lode in Nevada. By the time he died in 1909 at the age of 81, he left behind not only a fortune estimated at $25 million, but also about a half-dozen former wives, and two other snubbed ladies who tried unsuccessfully to kill him.[23] He has been described as a "lecherous, cigar smoking, card playing and blasphemous" high roller, but he was also a very successful, if extravagant, businessman.[24] In the course of his long life he pioneered in real estate developments around Lake Tahoe and built the Santa Anita race track on his California ranch, so he could run his thoroughbreds.

One of Baldwin's most spectacular enterprises was the hotel he built in San Francisco, which he named for himself. He was proud to call the Baldwin the finest hotel west of New York City, but the $3.5 million building burned to the ground in November 1898. When he went to Nome in 1900 there were rumors that he was broke.[25] Before the Baldwin Hotel had burned down, it had one of the longest bars in the United States. Lucky brought with him to Nome the heavy mahogany doors that had "once swung to and fro in the Baldwin annex, San Francisco," and he installed them on his more modest drinking establishment in Nome.[26]

The Baldwin on Front Street in Nome was housed in a relatively small building covered with corrugated iron, but inside it was described as "one of the finest drinking and gambling saloons in Nome." The bar fixtures were all of mahogany, a large mirror hung over the back of the bar, and the stained-glass windows "shed a dim irreligious light."[27] In addition Baldwin had shipped to Nome the finest piano in town, because he hoped to stage shows in the saloon, or to build a theater next door. His

mailmen's suits with them to Nome, thinking they would make good outfits in which to mine for gold. Instead of mining on the beach, however, they put on their uniforms and began their rounds in the city, to the amazement of everyone who saw them, as Lockley explained years later.

> The appearance of a uniformed letter carrier delivering mail as calmly in the midst of all the confusion as though at home was a sight that stopped traffic almost as quickly as a fight would have done. Men bent beneath the weight of a heavy pack would stop a moment, shift their packstraps and look at me. "That is the most natural thing I have seen since I left Denver," said one onlooker. "Blamed if it don't make a man feel as if he was in God's country and that Alaska was part of the United States."[20]

Lockley had numerous saloons on his route, which was understandable because saloons were said to be "almost as plentiful as goldseekers."[21] There were reportedly more than one hundred saloons and gambling houses in Nome.[22] Many of them were among the finest and biggest piano player could "make it hum with melody ranging in choice and compass from operatic selections to 'Just as the Sun Went Down,' 'Because I Love You,' and kindred ballads."[28]

Not everyone enjoyed the finer attributes of saloon life in Nome. When letter carrier Fred Lockley made his rounds in Nome during the summer of 1900, many of the saloon-keepers on his route offered him free drinks. "The quality of much of the Nome liquor was enough to make an ardent prohibitionist of a confirmed drunkard," Lockley claimed. Perhaps he was not qualified to be a judge, however, as he neither smoked nor drank. On one particularly hot and dusty day he accepted a saloon-man's offer of a free drink, and asked for a glass of boiled water. Lockley said he could hardly stand the look of scorn on the barkeeper's face, as he poured the mailman a beer glass of water. He never accepted the offer of a free drink again.[29]

The most unusual saloon in Nome was probably Dick Dawson and Charlie Suter's Second Class Saloon. Across the top of the door a large sign said: "The Only Second Class Saloon in Alaska." They called it the Second Class because as Dick Dawson often explained, "every saloon man in Alaska advertises his joint as the only first class saloon, so Charlie and myself decided to call ours the only 'second class saloon in Alaska.'"[30]

Upstairs above the saloon they had a 26-room hotel, "where all the comforts of modern civilization can be enjoyed." The floors were covered with Brussels carpets, each room had an electric call bell, and there were electric lights "to give brilliancy to the general effect." Dawson and Suter believed that one final detail made their rooms especially desirable. "Particular regard has been given to sanitary arrrangements," the *Nome Gold Digger* stated. "A large sewer has been put in extending from the rear of the building to tide water, and this sewer will be flushed every twenty-four hours."[31]

Sanitary facilities for most of those in Nome were not so convenient. Since the first gold seekers had arrived

Dick Dawson and Charlie Suter's famed Second Class Saloon. (Ethel Becker)

CALIFORNIA BAKERY CAFÉ
GOOD BREAD AND PASTRY.

THE BEST 25 AND 50¢ MEAL IN TOWN
GOOD COFFEE A SPECIALTY.

Museum of History and Industry

ENTREPRENEURS

Anyone with a tent and an empty spot on the ground could hang up a shingle and open a business in Nome, whether it was a saloon, a bank, or an architectural firm, like J.T. Cosgrove on the right. However, shops like the California Bakery Cafe (left), or the Golden Gate Store (below), offering dry goods, notions, and a circulating library, were more elaborate establishments.

Bancroft Library

Anchorage Historical and Fine Arts Museum

at Nome in 1898 and 1899, sanitation on the poorly drained tundra had been the most serious problem facing the community. Because the ground was frozen, waste water stayed on the surface of the tundra and did not drain away. The Nome Chamber of Commerce, which was the only local body with a semblance of authority after the Nome consent government of 1899 went bankrupt, had raised money to dig drainage ditches in the city during the spring of 1900.

Yet after navigation in the Bering Sea opened in May, and thousands of newcomers began to arrive in Nome,

the residents of the city were overwhelmed by the magnitude of the problems caused by the rapid increase in the population.[32]

The filthiest part of the community was behind the large saloons and false-front buildings on the main street of Nome, where the prostitutes' cribs were located. The chief army surgeon in Nome described the situation.

In the center of the town back of the principal saloons and in the district occupied by the prostitutes the conditions were simply vile; pools of stagnant water, slops, and

Along the Nome waterfront public closets were built on pilings, and the toilets were flushed when the tide came in. (Bancroft Library)

70

urine stood upon the surface with scarcely a possibility of drainage into the sea, there being but one or two narrow alleys in this compact line of houses, and where such a space did exist it merely became a common urinal. To pass dry-shod above this mass of filth, straw, paper, and other packing material, with a fair proportion of discarded wearing apparel and bedding, had been thrown to decompose and to be trampled under foot.[33]

An added danger was the threat of a smallpox epidemic. Numerous cases of the dreaded disease had appeared among the passengers on the ships that had come to Nome, and Lieutenant D.H. Jarvis of the revenue cutter service, the equivalent of the modern-day Coast Guard, ordered several large vessels including the *Ohio* and the *Santa Anna* into quarantine for about two weeks at Egg Island near Saint Michael, before they were permitted to unload their passengers. Also, a "pest house" was built one and a half miles outside of Nome to isolate those who had already landed in the city and had the highly contagious disease.[34]

The crisis came closer every day, and it was feared that an epidemic of typhoid fever, pneumonia, or smallpox might sweep through the city killing hundreds or thousands of men who were crowded together without adequate shelter or sanitary facilities. When Gen. George Randall arrived at Nome in late June 1900, the Nome Chamber of Commerce asked him to declare martial law. Unless the army took over the town, they feared that disease and lawlessness in the city would bring total chaos. "At request of Chamber of Commerce have assumed control of affairs in town of Nome...," General Randall informed his superiors in Washington, D.C., on June 26. "Estimated this date, 16,000 people in the town, and no effective civil organization for protection of life and property."[35]

Randall ordered everyone in Nome to clean up their own property, and appointed several health inspectors to enforce his orders. If a property owner did not pick up the garbage and remove the filth from his lot, then an armed guard was placed on the site until he did so. The general ordered that at least a half-dozen "closets" for the use of the public be constructed, and located over the water "far enough out to allow the tide to do the cleansing work."[36] He also established a regular military patrol on the streets of the city to enforce quarantine and sanitation regulations.

General Randall intended to keep the city under military rule only until newly appointed district judge Arthur H. Noyes arrived in several weeks. The judge could settle the hundreds of bitter disputes over mining property and town lots, and he could also oversee the establishment of a legally organized local government. The Alaska Code that had just been passed by Congress on June 6, 1900, enacted many long overdue reforms, including a provision that for the first time enabled Alaskan communities of more than three hundred residents to incorporate. The weaknesses of the consent government and the gold rush to Nome had demonstrated the critical need of legalizing local municipal governments in Alaska. The congressional legislation also recognized that more than one district judge was needed to govern Alaska, and created two new judgeships, with one of the new judicial seats at Eagle near the Canadian border on the Yukon River, and another at Saint Michael near the mouth of the Yukon.

Arthur H. Noyes was the new judge chosen to sit at Saint Michael in the Second Judicial Division, which included the Nome gold fields and most of northwestern Alaska. Judge Noyes arrived at Nome in mid-July 1900, and he did anything but establish law and order in Nome. Noyes was to play a key role in one of the greatest frauds in the history of American jurisprudence and one of the darkest chapters in the history of Alaska. His arrival at Nome on July 19, 1900, marked the beginning of the reign of "the Spoilers."

Chapter V
The Wickedest City

f ever a town needed law enforcement, it was gold rush Nome. One businessman estimated that a full third of the population of the gold rush town were idlers and footloose wanderers who "never do well anywhere under any circumstances," while another third were of the "sporting class," including gamblers and prostitutes.[1]

Every saloon attracted hordes of criminals, confidence men, and others looking for an easy dollar. "There never was a harder crowd herded together than was to be found here during the first few weeks following the opening of navigation," the *Nome Daily Chronicle* admitted in September 1900.[2] As early as November 1899, the North West Mounted Police had warned United States Army officials stationed along the Yukon River that many undesirable characters, many of whom were "among the worst criminals ever known on this continent," were en route from Dawson City to the golden beaches at Nome. The Mounties supplied a list of the known crooks headed to Nome and described the "special criminal vocations" of each. All of the military posts on the Yukon were ordered to keep an eye out for the following men:

H.M. CARR — Curley Carr, Prize fighter, has just done a term of six months in Dawson for vagrancy.

SAMMY DEERING — has several short sentences for theft in the U.S.

FRED WELSH — alias Big Fred; clever confidence man and general crook, and ex-member of "Soapy Smith's" gang.

JACK KERWIN — Gambler, was one of the leaders of the Bull Hill riots.

DOC WEST — all round crook and clever pickpocket.

SAM BERRY — gambler and all round crook.

STEVE McNICHOLS — general crook, has a bad record in Butte, Montana.

PAUL and W.H. STACKHOUSE — or Reardon Brothers, ex-members of O'Leary gang of Skagway.

BASTOW PAGE — [illegible] and all round crook, was sent out of Dawson.

NICK BURKHARDT — New York thief and confidence man; has been ordered out of a great many cities of the U.S.

C.B. HEATH — alias Hobo Kid; general crook, clever poker player, will mostly [sic] likely be found living with a dance hall girl by the name of....

SAM BELL — was connected with Jim Marshall's gang of train robbers of California.

ED RAMSEY — all round crook.

JAMES POUNCE — sneak thief, has just completed a term in Dawson for theft.

TOM FISK — all round crook, ex-member of "Soapy Smith's" gang.

BILL DOHERTY — general tough, killed a man in Boise, Idaho, and two men in Butte, Montana.

PADDY MacDONALD — all round crook.

TOM TRIGGS — general tough, has been in several shooting scrapes in the U.S.; used to travel with Doherty.

HANK FREIZE — gambler; runs a sure thing game.

ED McDONALD and ED ROSS — sneak thieves.

FRANK BULIVE — gambler and all round crook.

ED REID — clever pickpocket.[3]

Nome was crowded with crooks and confidence men. According to one authority, the city was the wildest in the west since Butte, Montana. (Bunnell Collection, University of Alaska Archives)

There were as many tough characters near every saloon door and street corner in Nome as there were in the underworlds of the largest cities in the country. Alfred H. Brooks, the eminent Alaskan geologist, said that Nome in 1900 was the only mining camp in Alaska or Yukon Territory where he ever had the slightest fear of being robbed, and it was the only city where he felt it necessary to carry a gun.[4]

Many others felt the same way. C.S.A. Frost, the attorney general's special agent in Nome, reported that the city was as lawless as any place he had ever seen. Frost summed up the situation for Attorney General John W. Griggs in early August 1900.

> To this place has flocked thousands of people attracted by the richness of the gold diggings, and thousands more have followed them to engage in every sort of business and scheme that would be liable to run into their pockets some of the proceeds of the miners' labor. With them have come some of the sharpest criminals, the most dangerous cutthroats and bad men that civilization has produced, and it is a conservative thing to say that Nome has within its limits the worst aggregation of criminals and unprincipled men and women that were ever drawn together in this country. The saloons and gambling houses and the narrow streets and dark alley ways along the beach offer every opportunity to this class of criminals [to] successfully engage in their practices.
>
> Compared with Nome, today Butte, Montana, which is famous as the wickedest city in the United States, is a righteous and law-abiding community.[5]

Despite the city's reputation, serious crimes in Nome did not happen every day, and the bodies of murdered men did not litter the streets each morning before breakfast. Nome's first cemetery, on the sand spit not far from the water's edge, was no boot hill. During the first 13 months in which records were kept, from September 1899 to October 1900, about a half-dozen murders were recorded in the city of Nome. Also during that time five men drowned and four committed suicide. Far more

deadly than the six-gun were pneumonia, typhoid fever, and tuberculosis, which killed most of the 87 people who died in Nome during that first year.[6]

There were few gun fights on the streets of Nome. "True there have been any number of hold-ups and robberies," the editor of the *Nome Daily Chronicle* wrote, "but street gun fighting, the thing that has given new mining camps the hard name they bear, has been almost unknown." The editor believed that the reason for the lack of shootouts was "the excellent discipline maintained by the military when the soldiers were in control."[7] For most of the summer civilian and military police patrolled the city, as one of the most famous gunfighters who ever lived found out on several occasions.

Wyatt Earp probably killed at least four men during his lifetime, including Frank Stilwell, Curly Bill, Indian Charlie, and John Ringo.[8] When Earp lived in Nome in 1899-1901, he was a slightly rotund, middle-aged saloonkeeper, and nearly 20 years had gone by since the famous shootout at the O.K. Corral. Earp and his partner C.E. Hoxsie ran the Dexter Saloon, and for the most part the old gunslinger was now a respectable businessman. A report in the *Seattle Post-Intelligencer* in the summer of 1900 explained that Earp, who had once operated a gambling house at 111 South Second in Seattle, had been carried northward by the rush to Nome, but had now "grown to like a quiet life."[9]

However, the 52-year-old saloon man was not enjoying the "quiet life" in the wee hours of June 29, 1900, when he got mixed up in a brawl on Front Street in Nome. Two drunks who had been fighting on the street were stopped by the arrival of two deputy marshals. When the marshals arrested one of the brawlers and started to take him to the jail in the army barracks, several other bystanders "forcibly effected" the release of the prisoner. One of those who helped free the prisoner was Wyatt Earp. When reinforcements arrived, the disorderly man was recaptured. "Wyatt Earp was likewise taken into custody," the *Nome Daily News* explained later in the

day. "He is charged with interfering with an officer while in the discharge of his duty." Earp maintained his innocence and claimed that he had been trying to assist the marshal and not to stop him.[10]

About a week later Wyatt's younger brother Warren was shot to death in Wilcox, Arizona. Warren Earp's murder has long been rumored to have been revenge for the part the Earp brothers had played at Tombstone in the early 1880s, when Wyatt, Virgil, and Morgan Earp, and their friend Doc Holliday, killed Billy Clanton and the two McLaury brothers at the O.K. Corral.[11] When the news reached Nome that another Earp brother had been gunned down, the *Arctic Weekly Sun* commented that

Wyatt, unlike his brothers, "seems inclined to break the record and die a natural death."[12] Despite that inclination, Earp was arrested again later in the summer of 1900, when he got involved in another barroom brawl. A military policeman stopped a slugfest in the Dexter Saloon, and took one man in for disorderly conduct. "The soldier, while performing this duty, was assaulted and beaten by Wyatt Earp and N. Marcus," a newspaper report stated in early September.[13]

Nome was probably the scene of more petty thievery, burglaries, and assaults, than any city of its size in the United States. "ROBBERS ARE RAMPANT," the Nome Gold Digger headlined in September 1900, and the newspaper warned its readers, "While the streets of Nome are absolutely safe during the day-time, by night citizens go forth knowing that the darkness is full of danger from thugs and footpads who infest this camp."[14]

An average day of crime in Nome usually included the robbing of several tents, which were easy pickings. The favorite modus operandi of criminals in Nome was to cut a slit through the canvas wall of a tent at night while the occupants were asleep, and with a capsule of chloroform attached to the end of a long pole, dump the knockout drug on their victims' heads.[15] Sometimes the technique did not work.

Mrs. M.W. Trevitt ran a women's clothing store in a tent on First Avenue, and she slept in the back of the tent. At four o'clock in the morning on Monday July 30, 1900, "she was awakened by the cold wind blowing in her face." There was the smell of chloroform in the air, and a gaping hole in her tent near the head of her cot. When she looked out through the hole in the canvas she saw a tall man whom she recognized as having visited her shop earlier that evening. She screamed and the would-be thief ran away.[16]

During the same night in another part of town Mr. A. J. Lindsay was walking back to his room at the Hotel Waldorf with a package of medicine from the Red Cross Drug Store. Suddenly two men jumped Lindsay and nearly killed him. "One of them hit him over the head with a sand bag," but he remembered nothing of what happened next. Somehow he stumbled back to his hotel "covered with mud and blood" and collapsed.[17]

Two cases of arson were also reported that evening, including a fire in a compound occupied by a group of Belgian prostitutes behind the Second Class saloon. Both fires were quickly extinguished and no one was hurt. More serious was a fight the night before in front of the Columbia Theatre between Daisy Staws, whom the Nome Daily News identified as "a lady of evil repute," and an unidentified man. Daisy and her suitor had a quarrel in front of the theater, and the dispute soon became violent. "Daisy hit the man with a hammer knocking him down," the Nome Daily News explained.

> She then ran inside the building. The man, picking himself up, drew a large sized gun and stooping down behind Sam Donnenbaum's cigar store, waited for the fair Daisy to reappear, so that he might bag her when she should emerge. Unfortunately for the sportsman's hopes, Daisy came out just as a soldier appeared and pulled both of them before any further damage could be done.[18]

Much of the crime in Nome was centered in the red-light district behind the saloons on the north side of Front Street, where most of the prostitutes' cribs were located. A high board fence was later constructed around the tenderloin, and it became known as the Restricted District or the Stockade. The prostitutes were semi-licensed by the authorities. Each woman had to pay a monthly "fine" of $10 or she would be arrested. This was a policy first started by the municipal consent government as a way of providing revenue. The police records of the consent government show that any number of gamblers and prostitutes were fined regularly each month.[19] "This was paid to the chief of police," a newspaper report explained, "and he and the municipal judge received their fees, the balance being turned into the city treasury."[20]

River Street along the Snake River, with the sternwheelers Los Angeles *and* City of Chicago *tied up along the bank.*
(Ethel Becker)

In early July a dispute arose between the United States commissioner at Nome and the municipal government over who should receive the lucrative prostitution and gambling "tax."[21] The issue became even more controversial when a deputy U.S. marshal made a raid on the tenderloin in mid-August, collecting $10 from each prostitute, and arresting several who refused to pay. The justification for the raid was that several attempts had been made in the tenderloin to burn down the city, and the marshal needed more money for fire protection, as well as extra funds to care for the destitute people in the city.[22]

C.S.A. Frost, the special representative of the U.S. Justice Department warned the marshal, "I know that the Attorney General and the government at Washington would not approve your action in this matter." Even if he did not have adequate funds to keep order in Nome, Frost said the marshal was "not authorized to impose a tax on an occupation prohibited by law in order to supply the deficiency."[23] Despite that fact however, fines for prostitution continued to be levied, and after the city of Nome was incorporated in 1901 the city council passed a tax of $11 a head on the women in the tenderloin.[24]

Many of the prostitutes and dance hall girls were as tough as any of the characters in Nome. "The women are either old maids or old married women and sports," one gold seeker bound for Nome had written.

> Most of the sports look pretty well worn out, and are looking for some place where competition will not put them so far in the shade, tho [sic] two young girls in our end of the boat are good looking, but know the ropes pretty well, from their actions.[25]

A grand jury investigation in September 1900 decided that most of the lawlessness in Nome was caused by the presence of women in the saloons and gambling houses. The grand jury found that "... much of the crime committed in Nome has been due to the fact that in

Alice Walker and Mabel McGilvery Brooks, who were on their way to Nome to sell insurance. (Carrie McLain Museum)

saloons and places of public resort, lewd and dissolute women are permitted to resort and congregate and there demean themselves like men."[26] The result was an order forbidding all women from saloons in Nome, except in

> . . . such resorts as have elevated stages [which] may employ vocalists and performers to entertain customers. But the women are not permitted to consort with men at the bar, or participate in the play at the gambling tables.[27]

The editor of the *Chronicle* thought that the new regulation prohibiting women from Nome's saloons was a good rule, "even if it serves no other purpose than to keep femininity from exposing its degradation to the public." As he explained, "Women have no place in saloons and their presence in such places is always followed by one sort of trouble or another."[28]

Yet the worst criminals in Nome were hardly the "lewd and dissolute" women who were acting like men in the saloons, or the thieves who chloroformed their victims in the tents on the beach. Far worse were the men who came to Nome from Washington, D.C., to enforce and to uphold the law. Rex Beach called them "the Spoilers."

"A grievous vision is declared unto me, the treacherous dealer dealeth treacherously, and the spoiler spoileth." So runs a line a from Isaiah. The most treacherous dealer of them all was Alexander ("the Great") McKenzie, the mastermind of a plot to steal millions of dollars of gold from the rightful owners of the richest claims in Nome. Even today, more than 80 years later, the enormity of the conspiracy is hard to comprehend. McKenzie was the Republican National Committeeman from North Dakota for 21 years, and he reportedly "knew personally every Republican President from Grant to Harding."[29] He was eventually sentenced to a year in prison for his part in the Nome conspiracy on a charge of contempt of court. Yet William McKinley, one of McKenzie's presidential friends, soon pardoned the North Dakota political boss on the grounds that McKenzie was in poor health and

Small boats ferried passengers across the mouth of the Snake River to the sand spit.
(Ethel Becker)

WOMEN OF NOME

*M*any of the women in Nome worked right alongside the men. Some mined the beach sands (right), while others such as this native woman (below) took in washing. Though only men were permitted to join the Nome Ski Club, these women (left) in full-length dresses enjoyed themselves nonetheless.

probably would not live out the remaining months of his term. When McKenzie died 20 years later, he took many of the inside details of the gold conspiracy with him to his grave, as he never wrote anything down on paper unless it was necessary.

Despite the thousands of pages of legal proceedings related to the case which survive in the record books, all the details of the plot are not totally clear, and probably never will be. It is certain, however, that in 1900, Alexander McKenzie, with the help of his puppet Arthur H. Noyes, almost pulled off one of the boldest frauds in American legal history.

The foundation for McKenzie's con game was the uncertainty as to whether or not aliens could legally stake mining claims. It was the same issue over which the miners in the Nome district had fought since the first discovery of gold. The prevailing belief in Nome was that Swedes, Lapps, Norwegians, and others who were not American citizens had illegally staked the richest mining claims in the district. Therefore they concluded that the property which these "foreigners" had claimed was still in the public domain and was open to staking by anyone who a citizen.

This theory was completely at odds with the law, which stated that the issue of citizenship could only be raised by the government itself when a man applied for a patent for his mining claim. Even if a foreigner did stake a mining claim he could later become a citizen or declare his intention to become a citizen, and then apply for a patent like any natural born American. No miner had the right to challenge the citizenship of another miner, or to use that as a pretext upon which to jump his claim. Hundreds of the miners who arrived on the scene after the original locators never accepted this as a fact, and they jumped every claim that they thought might have been staked by a foreigner.[30]

In 1900 most of the richest claims on Anvil Creek were owned by the two largest mining companies in Nome: the Pioneer Mining Company, which represented the original discoverers of the Nome district, and Charles D. Lane's Wild Goose Mining and Trading Company. On the other hand many of the "jumpers' titles" to those rich claims had been purchased by the Nome law firm of Hubbard, Beeman, and Hume, which hoped to get control of any claims that had been staked "illegally" by aliens, or could otherwise be challenged in court.

Rich mining claims on Anvil Creek were the prime target of Alexander McKenzie and the Spoilers.
(Ethel Becker)

Clean up on No. 1 Below Discovery, Anvil Creek.
(Ethel Becker)

During the winter of 1899-1900, while thousands of respectable people were planning to leave for Nome as soon as possible, Alexander McKenzie was making a few plans of his own. By that time Anvil Creek had been proven to be incredibly rich, and McKenzie saw a chance to make a fortune over the issue of whether or not the alien claims on Anvil were valid. In the early months of 1900 he formed the Alaska Gold Mining Company, a syndicate capitalized on paper at $15 million, and purchased many of the jumpers' titles that Hubbard, Beeman, and Hume controlled, and others.

McKenzie was the president of the Alaska Gold Mining Company, and he retained 51 percent of the stock for himself and several influential friends in Washington, D.C., including among others, Sen. Henry C. Hansborough of North Dakota, and Sen. Thomas Carter of Montana. McKenzie's syndicate reportedly owned about five hundred titles to mining claims in the Nome area.[31] Most of these were jumpers' titles and they would not be worth anything until the claims of the original locators were invalidated. McKenzie tried to have Congress attach an amendment to the Alaska Code, which was then under consideration on Capitol Hill, that would retroactively nullify any mining claims in Alaska that had been staked by aliens. By wiping the slate clean of "alien locations" McKenzie's own jumpers' titles would automatically be worth millions.

Charles D. Lane had paid $300,000 for four claims on Anvil Creek, three of which had been staked by Lapps. He was also spending a half-million dollars to build a piping system to bring water to his claims so they could be mined on a large scale, and to construct a narrow-

gauge railroad to his property. Under the mining laws as they stood when he bought the claims, his investment was protected. With McKenzie's scheme, however, he stood to lose every penny.

Despite the valiant efforts of Senator Hansborough, Senator Carter, and McKenzie's other friends in Washington, D.C., the "McKenzie amendment" to the Alaska Code was defeated, thanks in part to the opposition of Charles D. Lane and others. Yet Alexander "the Great" did not give up easily, and he thought of a new plan to get what he wanted.

Congress passed the Alaska Code on June 6, 1900, creating two new judgeships in Alaska. Because of the lack of other government officials, the judges in each district had great authority and administrative and judicial power. McKenzie sized up the situation and he decided that the appointment of a friendly judge in Nome would be the easiest way of lining his pockets with other men's gold. Using his connections with wealthy financiers and leading Republican politicians, he pushed through the appointment of Arthur N. Noyes, an undistinguished Minnesota attorney and a longtime crony of McKenzie's, as judge of the new Second Judicial Division of Alaska, which included the Nome gold fields.

Noyes was hardly qualified for the position. He drank too much, and even McKenzie was sometimes disappointed that he had so little character. But he did do everything that McKenzie told him to do, and that made Noyes a perfect choice for the position.

On July 19, 1900, Noyes and McKenzie arrived in the Nome roadstead on the steamship *Senator*. Within four days Alexander McKenzie was in control of a half-dozen of the richest placer mining claims in the district, and was working the claims as if he owned them. The basic plan was simple. The law firm of Hubbard, Beeman, and Hume filed complaints with Judge Noyes disputing the legality of the original locations of the richest claims on Anvil Creek, then being mined by the Pioneer Mining Company and the Wild Goose Mining and Trading

Taking a ride on the Wild Goose Railroad. (Ethel Becker)

The end of track on Anvil Creek. (Ethel Becker)

Company. The judge then granted an injunction, evicting the rightful owners from their property, and appointed McKenzie as a receiver for the claims, to mine the gold from the ground while the question of ownership was being litigated.

McKenzie was far from an impartial outsider and utterly unfit to serve as an agent of the court in the case. The receiver was supposed to protect the interests of both the plaintiff and the defendant, but as the president of the Alaska Gold Company he was secretly one of the plaintiffs himself. Of course there was no valid reason to have a receiver in a mining claim dispute in the first place, because the receiver's only duty was to protect the value of the property while the issues were being contested in court. The gold would have been far safer in the ground than it was in the hands of McKenzie.

Judge Noyes and receiver McKenzie flagrantly violated numerous laws in setting up their operation. McKenzie worked the mines and took out thousands of dollars each day. He reportedly gutted several of them, while Noyes stonewalled the rightful owners of the claims, forbidding them from stepping on the property that was theirs. The attorneys for the Pioneer Mining Company and the Wild Goose Mining and Trading Company asked the district court to lift the injunctions and remove McKenzie as receiver, but the motions were denied by Judge Noyes. They then asked to appeal the cases to the circuit court of appeals in San Francisco, but again their requests were denied. With no legal recourse left for them in Nome, the attorney for the defendants sent their petitions directly to the circuit court in San Francisco by steamship, hoping to find the justice that had been denied them in Nome.

In late August 1900, Judge William Morrow of the Ninth Circuit Court of Appeals reviewed the briefs and petitions of the attorneys from the Pioneer and Wild Goose Mining companies. It was immediately apparent to him that both Noyes and McKenzie had "grossly abused" their power.[32] He issued a write of *supersedeas* and immediately ordered the injunctions to be lifted. He

WORKING FOR WAGES

Working men in the Nome gold fields earned their pay. They put in long hours, under poor conditions, and most were thousands of miles from home. Whether digging in an underground drift mine (left), sluicing on topside (below), or working on the railroad (right), a pick and shovel man didn't easily make a fortune in Alaska.

Anchorage Historical and Fine Arts Museum

Ethel Becker

dismissed McKenzie as the receiver and ordered him to return all of the property he had seized.

When Morrow's orders were brought back to Nome on September 14, 1900, they hit the McKenzie camp like a "bombshell." [33] But McKenzie was only momentarily stunned. "Nobody can hurt me," he had bragged to his followers about his power in Washington, D.C. "I am too strong at headquarters!" [34] McKenzie ignored the orders from the circuit court, while Judge Noyes meekly claimed that he was powerless to stop McKenzie because the issue was no longer under his jurisdiction. Both McKenzie's henchmen, as well as the followers of Lane and Lindeberg, armed themselves, hired detectives to spy on the enemy, and prepared for bloodshed.

When McKenzie defied the orders of the circuit court, an armed posse from the Pioneer Mining Company drove off the receiver's cronies from several claims on Anvil Creek. The military forces in Nome, who were caught between the crooked judiciary and the outraged citizens, tried their best to keep the peace. At a conference held in the army barracks between the two sides after the battle on Anvil Creek, McKenzie and William H. Metson, the leading attorney for the Pioneer Mining Company, came face to face. After trading insults and accusations, they nearly killed each other.

"We both went after our guns," Metson said later. "I instantly figured that as I had a small caliber I would have to shoot him through the head to stop him. Just as I was about to pull the trigger the soldiers got me. McKenzie was left handed and had just gotten his gun out of his pocket when they grabbed him." [35]

Again attorneys for Lane and Lindeberg sailed south to San Francisco with the information that McKenzie had refused to obey the orders of the circuit court, and that Noyes had refused to enforce them. It was now a race against time, as navigation would close by late October or early November. If further word was not received from the circuit court by then, McKenzie's reign of terror might last for another year.

On the morning of October 15, 1900, two deputy marshals from California landed in Nome from the steamship *Oregon,* with orders to enforce the earlier writs of the circuit court. They also had a warrant for the arrest of Alexander McKenzie. He was charged with contempt of court, and the two marshals came to take him to San Francisco to stand trial. The two California lawmen found him eating breakfast at the Golden Gate Hotel. Though at first he said that no "so and so" was going to arrest him, on the advice of his lawyer he surrendered. The nightmare that had started with McKenzie's arrival at Nome three months earlier was nearly over. That night on Anvil Creek the mine owners and operators fired their guns in the air, as if it was the Fourth of July, and celebrated the end of McKenzie's tyrannical rule. [36]

McKenzie was convicted of contempt of court in 1901, and was sentenced to a year in prison. [37] After serving three months and two weeks in jail, President McKinley pardoned the North Dakota Republican boss because of his failing health. A few hours later astonished observers saw a suddenly rejuvenated McKenzie sprinting across the railroad depot trying to catch the first train out of Oakland. [38]

Arthur H. Noyes never went to prison. He officially remained as judge of the Second Judicial Division of Alaska until 1902, when he was convicted of contempt of court, fined $1,000, and removed from office by Pres. Theodore Roosevelt. [39] Several other lesser lights in the McKenzie-Noyes ring did go to jail, however, including C.S.A. Frost, the investigator for the attorney general's office who had been shocked by the number of cutthroats, thieves, and criminals in Nome.

McKenzie's plan ultimately failed because Noyes was so incompetent as a judge, and his actions so irregular, while McKenzie himself was too bold and brazen in his defiance of standard legal procedures. He took out about $600,000 in gold during his reign as receiver, though it appears that his ultimate plan was to make millions more by selling stock in his Alaska Gold Mining Company to

The raw gold from the creeks around Nome was melted down into bars at the Bank of Cape Nome. (Ethel Becker)

GOLD BRICKS
345-G
BANK OF CAPE NOME, NOME, ALASKA.

Rex Beach was second only to Jack London as a gold rush novelist. His first work of fiction, and one of his best sellers, was The Spoilers. *(Lomen Collection, University of Alaska Archives)*

The story of McKenzie's rule in Nome was one of the most dramatic episodes in Alaskan history, especially when set against the backdrop of the Nome stampede. Rex Beach, who along with Robert Service and Jack London was one of the three most famous literary figures of the northern gold rushes, came to Nome in 1900. He lived under McKenzie's reign and launched his career as a novelist with a book called *The Spoilers*. It was a romantic novel based on McKenzie's skullduggery, and though Beach went on to write more than 30 books, it was one of the most popular he ever published. Ten years after it appeared in 1906, *The Spoilers* had sold close to eight hundred thousand copies, and it has been republished more than a half-dozen times since.[41] In addition the novel was made into a movie five times between 1914 and 1955, with stars such as Marlene Dietrich, John Wayne, Gary Cooper, Rory Calhoun, William Boyd, and Randolph Scott cast in various versions of the screen epic.[42]

For several years the mass of complicated legal challenges, which sprang from the reign of the Spoilers, hindered the systematic development of the mines in the Nome region. Yet despite the unfavorable legal climate, the total gold production on the Seward Peninsula in 1900 was close to $5 million. The three greatest-producing streams were Anvil Creek, Glacier Creek, and Dexter Creek. By far the richest was Anvil Creek. Even with the legal wrangling over the Anvil Creek claims, the miners on that stream took out $1,750,000 in placer gold during the season of 1900.[43]

However, few of the thousands of gold seekers at Nome in 1900 ever came close to a gold mine. As English mining engineer Arthur L. Pearse put it, gold rush Nome, for a "so-called mining camp, was remarkably devoid of mining men." The gamblers, speculators, and "sidewalk miners" that filled the streets of Nome had no desire to use a pick or a shovel.[44] "Never was there seen such an exodus of schemers, all with a fortune-breeding plan," the *Seattle Post-Intelligencer* said of those who went to

unwary investors, after the rich production from "his" mines in 1900. No one was ever really punished for the conspiracy itself, only for contempt of court. A conspiracy trial was never held. As W.E. Lillo, the leading historian of the Spoilers, wrote many years ago, "the manner in which the promoters of this enterprise escaped the vengeance of the law has no parallel in the crime annals of the country."[40]

Nome. "These men engaged in a gamble; win or lose they have no complaint due."[45]

In the midst of the gold rush unemployed men walked the streets of Nome as if it were the bottom of a depression. The appeals for relief from the indigent overwhelmed the churches. Hundreds of men had come to Nome with literally no money in their pockets, hoping to get rich quick picking gold up off the beach. "They came expecting gold to shower upon them in the same miraculous manner that manna fell upon the Israelites in the desert," the *Nome News* said of the worst charity cases. "Such a contingency as poverty never entered into their calculations."[46]

But there was neither manna, nor very much gold left on the Nome beach. By June 1900 it looked like the world's longest junkyard. "Now there is a lot of jackass machinery in this country," the *Nome News* reported on June 23, "and there is more on the way. Most of it will lie on the beach sands and its rotting timbers and rusting iron will only be left to tell the tale of overconfidence and misdirected energy and money."[47]

Pumps, pipes, steam engines, rockers, long toms, treadmills, bucket dredges, and sluice boxes lined the shore. According to one newspaper count, about eight thousand men were mining the beach by late July 1900, using three hundred to four hundred different types of gold digging machines. "In fact," the *Nome Gold Digger* reported, "the plants are as wonderful an evidence of American push and inventive genius as can be cited. Men have put their money into the most ingenious and most ridiculous schemes."[48]

One man walked a treadmill which not only pumped water but also shook his rocker, and according to the *Nome News* several "modern Don Quixotes" set up small windmills to pump water into their sluice boxes. Though it was obvious that most of the machines were useless, the *News* had to admit, "The contraptions . . . are wonderful to behold."[49]

Even those contraptions that would have actually worked, however, had arrived on the scene too late. By the time the rush of gold seekers had arrived at Nome in the summer of 1900, the beach sands had been worked

A mechanical monster on the Nome beach. (University of Washington Library)

THE GOLD EXTRACTORS

*I*t was widely believed in 1900 that the gold in the sand at Nome came in with the tide, and had been washed ashore by ocean currents. Many extravagant and impractical dredges such as the one on the right were constructed at great expense to mine the "countless millions" that were thought to lie on the bottom of the Bering Sea. This machine, like many others, was quickly destroyed in the rough surf (below), and the remains rusted away on the sands they had been built to mine. Other strange-looking mining contraptions, such as the pedal operated water wheel on the left, were less costly failures.

Arwine Company

Arwine Company

A two-man-powered sluicing
plant on the Nome beach.
(Ethel Becker)

over by thousands of miners half a dozen times, and the "inexhaustible" supply of gold in the sand was running out. Beach mining had gone on all winter long, with miners sluicing the gold out of the sand inside their tents or cabins, and most of the gold was already gone.

It was estimated that every dollar's worth of gold that the stampeders mined on the Nome beach in 1900 cost the men who earned it at least two dollars or more. The thousands of miners on the beach in 1900 may have spent from $3 million to $6 million on mining equipment, while the total gold production on the beach for the season was only about $350,000.[50]

The most spectacular failures were the machines designed to dredge the sand beneath the sea. "These projects were launched on the flimsiest sort of evidence that the sought-for gold existed at all," one newspaper report stated.[51] About 20 dredges, some of which had cost thousands of dollars apiece, were abandoned almost immediately by their owners, proving beyond a doubt that the bottom of the Bering Sea was not covered with gold.

The largest of the beach dredges looked like prehistoric mechanical monsters. They were mounted on huge steel wheels or rollers, enabling them to be pulled into the surf, so that their long-necked suction pumps could suck up the sand beneath the surface of the water. Some of the huge dredges were so heavy that they could hardly move, and for years after the gold rush several dredges of "nightmarish design" could be seen abandoned on the Nome beach, half-buried in the sand which they had been built to mine. The most uneconomical dredge might have been the Red Elephant, which had been built right on the beach at a cost of about $30,000. According to one account a 15-man crew operated the Red Elephant in the shallow water off the beach for a few days and reportedly took out 90¢ worth of gold.[52]

Even if the sea bottom had been covered with gold, most of the dredges and expensive mining machinery installed on the beach would have probably failed anyway, because such machines could not operate under the harsh weather conditions on the shores of the Seward Peninsula. As one writer explained at the time, "there are few places in the world where there is an uglier surf more days in the year than on the coast of western Alaska."[53] There were several bad storms which struck the coast during the summer, but the final blow for the beach miners came from the series of storms which swept across Nome in early September 1900. Towering waves and winds of up to 75 miles an hour destroyed or washed away almost everything on the beach, and a good part of Nome's business district as well.

The total damage was estimated at nearly $750,000. At the height of the storm on September 12 several buildings had to be tied down to keep them from washing away, and many more were tossed into the air by the waves and smashed to pieces.[54]

Hundreds of men were truly destitute after the storm, and they returned to the states as penniless refugees on army transport ships. They were just a small part of the massive exodus of about 15,000 disappointed gold seekers which left Nome by the close of the season.[55]

A few of them were looking for new adventures. When the news of the Boxer Rebellion reached Nome, a rough-and-tumble fighter known as Denver Ed Smith helped set up a recruiting office near the Horseshoe Saloon, asking for volunteers. Eventually 103 Nome men signed a petition and sent it to Alaska governor John G. Brady, offering to fight the "frenzied mobs of Chinamen in the city of Pekin, China." Governor Brady declined their offer.[56]

The Nome gold rush ended in September 1900 as quickly as it had begun three months earlier. As the waters receded on September 13, one correspondent thought that the beach was "now as level and as smooth as if there had never been any gold in Alaska, and the great Nome rush were but a figment of the imagination."[57] Not until 60 years later did the U.S. census record an Alaskan city with a population equal to that which Nome had during the wild summer of 1900.[58]

Waves threatening the tents on the sand spit, before the September 1900 storm. (Paul Mogensen and Mark Hufstetler)

SAND SPIT
BEFORE THE LATE STORM
Sept 12, 1900.

W. Hester, Photo.
Seattle

Before the storm in the fall of 1900, boats and tents lined the sand spit, and a large floating dredge was anchored just outside the mouth of the Snake River. (Howard Hein)

After the storm had subsided, almost everything, including the sand spit itself, had washed away. (Howard Hein)

On the Beach — Nome, Alaska, Oct. 14th, 1904.

Chapter VI
After the Gold Rush

The city of Nome has always lived in the memory of the 1900 stampede. Never has the population of the city come close to equaling the number of people in Nome during the gold rush. The events of the crazy summer of 1900 were not repeated in 1901, but the population of the town remained more or less stable at about five thousand through the early years of this century.

The easily worked beach diggings had been largely exhausted by 1900, but the mining industry on the Seward Peninsula continued to develop. The legal situation in the Nome mining district gradually improved as the litigation and lawsuits regarding the richest mining claims were slowly resolved under the leadership of Judge James Wickersham, who replaced Noyes. Gold production on the Seward Peninsula remained steady between 1900 and 1905 at about $4 million or $5 million a year, most of which was from the Nome region. The peak years of placer gold production were 1906 and 1907, when miners worked the famous Third Beach Line, and produced almost $15 million in two years. The Third Beach was one of a series of about a half-dozen "ancient beaches" discovered far beneath the surface of the tundra. Alfred Brooks and F.C. Schrader, the first geologists in the region, had predicted that ancient submerged beach lines, which had marked the edge of the sea in past ages, might be as rich as the modern-day ocean beach had been. No one paid much attention to the men in "khaki-pants," but million-dollar discoveries by J.C. Brown and Sam Samson on the Third Beach Line in 1904 and 1905 proved the great wealth of the ground.[1]

Where the gold was found at a relatively shallow depth in the tundra, miners used hydraulic techniques, firing streams of water to break down and mine the gravel. Deeper deposits were tapped by sinking narrow shafts sometimes hundreds of feet through the frozen ground to bedrock, thawing the ground every inch of the way with open fires or steam boilers. Once the shaft had reached bedrock, the miners dug drifts out in either direction searching for the pay streak. When the drift miners found rich gravel, they excavated crosscut tunnels throughout the extent of their claim, and hauled all the dirt to the surface by a hand-cranked windlass or a steam-powered hoist. Much of this underground work could be done during the winter, but they had to wait until early summer to run the huge "dump" of pay dirt through a sluice box to wash out the gold.

A tremendous volume of water was needed to mine gold on a large scale and the mine operators on the Seward Peninsula built a network of ditches totaling hundreds of miles to carry water to the mines on the creeks. One visionary remarked that from outer space the mines on the creeks would probably look like the canals on Mars, but the ditches, though costly, seemed like a sound investment. During the first decade of mining on the Seward Peninsula, the total gold production was nearly $50 million, most of which was mined from the Nome district.[2] Gold production started to decline steadily after the Third Beach was worked out in 1907, but the future still looked bright. In 1908 the Geological Survey calculated that there were 725 miles of gold-bearing streams on the Seward Peninsula, and that a conservative estimate of the total placer gold reserves of the region was between $250 million and $325 million.[3]

On the foundation of an estimated quarter-billion dollars in gold, the city of Nome prospered for a few years

A quiet fall day on the beach at Nome, October 10, 1904.
(Bancroft Library)

*Tex Rickard, the man who built Madison Square Garden, ran the
Northern Saloon in Nome, which is all decked out in honor of Adm.
George Dewey, the hero at the battle of Manila.* (Bunnell Collection,
University of Alaska Archives)

as the largest city in Alaska. Even after it had been passed by Fairbanks in both population and gold production in about 1905-6 Nome remained the "metropolis" of the Seward Peninsula and northwestern Alaska.

When first given the chance in November 1900, the people of Alaska's largest city refused to create an official city government and voted 384 to 311 not to incorporate the town of Nome.[4] Most Nome residents soon regretted that decision. During the winter of 1900-1901 committees of the Nome Chamber of Commerce tried to provide health, police, and fire protection for the city, but the job was too big for a volunteer organization. In April 1901, another vote was held and this time incorporation passed by an overwhelming margin.[5]

A city council was also elected at the same time, and included among these first, official city fathers were Charlie Hoxsie, Wyatt Earp's partner in the Dexter Saloon, and George Lewis ("Tex") Rickard, one of the owners of the Northern Saloon. Twenty years later Tex Rickard was the most famous boxing promoter in the world, and the pioneer of the million-dollar gate. When he died in 1929 he lay in state in Madison Square Garden, the house Rickard built for boxing.[6]

Rickard had landed at Nome in June 1899 and his Northern Saloon was one of the landmarks of the city. He always knew how to put on a show. His party for the poor people of Nome on Christmas Day 1900 was legendary. He and his partners footed the bill for about seven hundred or eight hundred turkey dinners for the "penniless and hungry men and women who could not afford a turkey of their own.'"[7] His generosity was not soon forgotten, and four months later Rickard was the leading vote getter in the election of Nome's first city government.

When Tex Rickard took office in 1901, Nome was changing fast, and soon it looked more like an established city than a frontier boom town. In the space of a few months Nome's first city council passed ordinances which made it illegal to drive dog teams within the city limits of Nome between June 1 and October 1, or to fire

Nome's first official city government. Standing from left to right are Bill McPhee, John Harris, S.H. Stevens, and Charlie Hoxsie. Seated from left to right are Tex Rickard, Mayor Julius Guise, and Capt. William Geiger. (University of Alaska Archives)

a gun or set off firecrackers without the permission of the mayor or the council. Prostitution was outlawed. The council also passed an ordinance similar to the 1900 rule forbidding women from "frequenting" saloons. In addition the council declared that anyone caught dealing or playing "faro, monte, roulette, twenty-one, poker, draw poker, bluff, crap, klondyke, black jack, or any banking or other game" would be fined up to $250 or given 60 days in jail, or both.[8]

The wild days in Nome were ending, but not overnight. Gambling, the favorite pastime of almost everyone in Nome, continued to flourish openly in the city. Like an early-day Las Vegas, the people of Nome would bet on anything including what day the first ship of the year would arrive in port, what day the last boat would leave, the outcomes of dog races, prize fights, basketball games, baseball games, the time of day, and the name of the president of the United States. A serious reform effort to wipe out gambling in Nome was begun in 1906, and a wave of police raids and arrests followed. The professional gamblers became more cautious and posted guards along the street and outside their card rooms. When authorities raided the back room of the Lacey barber shop in 1907, they seized faro, panguingue, and poker outfits, but most of the gamblers made their get-away through a secret trap door in the floor of the shop leading to the beach that had been installed for just such an emergency.[9]

A prize fight in Nome. Most such bouts were brutal affairs.
(Carrie McLain Museum)

The gaslit pool hall of the Board of Trade Saloon.
(Carrie McLain Museum)

The favorite sport of the gamblers and many other Nome residents in the early years of the city was prize fighting, and thousands of dollars were often wagered on a Friday night bout. Nome had more than its share of boxing greats. Besides Tex Rickard, some of the other students of the sweet science in Nome included Doc Kearns, one of the most successful boxing managers of all time who later handled Jack Dempsey, and Tommy Burns, the heavyweight champion of the world from 1906 to 1908.[10]

Prize fights in Nome were usually staged in rings set up in saloons or theaters, and some were especially brutal. "Hard hitting was the rule," stated one account of a 16-round battle between the Liverpool Kid and Kid Harris, "and gore bespattered the fighters and floor in quantities sufficient to satisfy the most blood-thirsty."[11] When Dick Case beat Ed Kelly in 12 rounds at the Standard Theatre, Kelly's "head was reduced to the consistency of a boiled melon."[12] In 1901 Nick Burley won the heavyweight championship of Nome by defeating Curly Carr in a bitter "fight to the finish" that lasted 25 rounds. "There were kidney blows, crosscounters, uppercuts and body and face punches galore," the *Nome Nugget* reported. "In fact, there was displayed everything known in the business and a few extras. The men were so angered with each other that twice during the evening the chief of police had to assist the referee in separating them during a clinch, and on one occasion, during a clinch, they spat in each others face."[13]

Boxing was a disreputable sport, not only because of the violence of the contests or the high stakes gambling associated with them, but also because many of the fighters were alleged to be as crooked as the streets of Nome. Sometimes the contestants signed contracts with one another beforehand dividing up the gate proceeds, and stipulating that their "fight to the finish" would go at least a certain number of rounds before they got serious. Other fights were outright fakes, rehearsed and staged like Shakespearian plays.[14]

When prize fighting and gambling were both outlawed,

Front St Nome Alaska, Before The Big Fire

they went underground, as did prostitution. The red-light district in Nome, the Stockade, stood behind the saloons on Front Street for seven years after the Nome city council officially declared prostitution illegal in the city of Nome in 1901. Every year religious leaders, reformers, newspaper editors, real estate owners, downtown businessmen, and city officials fought over the issue of whether or not the prostitutes' small cribs behind the high board fence of the Stockade should be moved to a more discreet location. The problem was that the Stockade was right in the heart of downtown Nome, and was much more open to the public gaze than red-light districts were supposed to be.

"For years," complained the editor of the *Nome Pioneer Press,* "have the young and old people of Nome been forced to pass and view the scenes which are the usual routine in what is known as the under world, and the moral injury which has been done from that one feature, alone, is almost beyond estimate."[15]

The reform movement to move the Stockade gained great momentum especially after the disastrous 1905 fire in Nome which started near the tenderloin district. The fire began at about three o'clock in the morning on September 13, 1905. Conflicting stories were told about the origin of the fire, but it probably started when a coal oil lamp overturned in a back room of the Alaska Saloon, or in a nearby cabin in the Stockade.[16] The fire spread quickly across the narrow confines of Front Street from one wooden building to the next, with tanks of gasoline exploding all the way down the street. By the time the fire was put out, it had gutted two blocks in the center of Nome, destroying about 50 businesses, including several saloons, restaurants, hotels, grocery stores, a bowling alley, and nearly 20 cabins in the Stockade.

"Of all the buildings on both sides of the street," a newspaper reporter said about Nome's business district, "scarcely a trace remains, save twisted corrugated iron and a few half burnt safes, warped and scorched."[17]

The 1905 fire was one of the worst in Nome's history,

though it was not nearly as disastrous as the 1934 blaze which nearly destroyed the entire community. No one was reported killed in the 1905 fire, and businessmen started to rebuild right away. Five of the burned saloons were reopened for business within three days of the fire, and they were soon followed by others.[18]

In the aftermath of the 1905 fire civic leaders launched a new campaign to move the Stockade out of downtown

Within days after the 1905 fire, the Second Class Saloon reopened for business. (Reprinted from The ALASKA JOURNAL®)

Nome's wood-paved Front Street before the 1905 fire. Behind the large saloons on the main street were the prostitutes' cribs in the Stockade, where the devastating fire started.
(National Maritime Museum)

Nome. No action was taken, however, and the Stockade remained in business behind Front Street, with the police occasionally making raids on the district, and arresting those who failed to pay the standard $5 or $10 a month fine.

Three years after the 1905 fire, under pressure from District Judge Alfred Moore, and other federal officials, the Stockade was finally abolished. The red-light fence was torn down during the night of June 2, 1908, and the prostitutes were forced to find other lodgings throughout the city.[19]

At first it was proposed that the old site of the Stockade could be made into a "public playground for the children of Nome."[20] As more families had settled in Nome, concerned citizens had long pointed out the need for a Nome city park with a few benches, graveled walks, and "a space of even tundra," where mothers could "perambulate" with their babies, and the sick could stroll peacefully in the fresh air.[21] Nome's city fathers decided, however, that the old site of the Stockade was too valuable as business property to be reserved for perambulating mothers, when the city of Nome itself was surrounded by miles of open tundra.

Though Nome did not have a park or a playground, most visitors were surprised at the modern conveniences that such an isolated community did have. Nome was a city with streetlights, an electric power plant, a local telephone exchange, and a long-distance telephone system that connected Nome with most of the mining camps scattered throughout the Seward Peninsula. The drinking water used in the city during the summer was supposedly "the purest water in the world," and was piped to the city through a wooden conduit five miles across the tundra from Moonlight Springs on Anvil Mountain.[22] The city also had a primitive sewage system that consisted of a few "main sewers" running downhill from the highest ground in the city to the Bering Sea.[23] During the winter garbage disposal was handled in a convenient fashion. After the ocean around Nome froze solid, the city health officer staked a line with red flags hundreds of feet out on the ice. All garbage had to be dumped on the ice beyond the "flag line." When the ice broke up in the spring, the garbage disappeared.[24]

Nome had Catholic, Episcopal, Methodist and Congregational churches. Saint Joseph's Catholic Church had a steeple about one hundred feet tall, which was about the tallest structure in the city of Nome. The steeple was topped by an electrically lighted six-by-eight-foot cross. The lighted cross served both believers and nonbelievers as a signal beacon to guide travelers caught out on the tundra during a blizzard, or lost at sea, and was maintained by the city government.[25]

The city of Nome had a "graded public school with seven teachers and 350 scholars."[26] The narrow streets of downtown Nome had several crowded business blocks with some buildings that were three stories tall. The city fire department did its best to keep them from burning down with equipment that included a modern steam-powered fire engine, which had cost $10,000. When the fire fighters placed the intake hose in the ocean or the Snake River (where open holes were kept from freezing during the winter to provide a water supply) the engine

A ticket good for eight buckets of water from the Nome Water Company. (Lomen Collection, University of Alaska Archives)

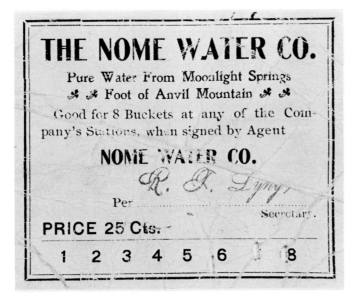

THE NOME WATER CO.

Pure Water From Moonlight Springs
❧ ❧ Foot of Anvil Mountain ❧ ❧

Good for 8 Buckets at any of the Company's Stations, when signed by Agent

NOME WATER CO.

R. J. Lynn,

Per _____

Secretary.

PRICE 25 Cts.

1 2 3 4 5 6 7 8

Digging out Steadman Avenue after a blizzard. At the end of the street is Saint Joseph's Catholic Church. The steeple was topped by an electric cross, which served as a beacon for lost travelers. (Powell Collection, University of Alaska Archives)

Leta Hamilton

ENTERTAINMENT

*F*or a small isolated community, Nome offered a wide variety of entertainment. In the summer traveling vaudeville shows (right) came through town, and the Nome Brass Band (below) was always ready for the Fourth of July and other festive occasions. When the city was icebound between October and June, home-grown talent had a chance to shine. A production of Gilbert and Sullivan's Mikado (left) by a local cast in April 1906 was a smash hit. "The big audience was generous in its applause," the Nugget reported, "and it demanded many encores. . . ."

Leta Hamilton

Golden Gate Hall

Sparkling, Refined Family

Vaudeville

Entertainment and Ball

WEDNESDAY EVENING, JULY 12

| J. W. CAMPBELL | - | Orchestra Leader |
| HARRY RIVERS | - - - | Stage Director |

PROGRAM

EDNA BURMEISTER
"I Have No Sweetheart But You,".............
....To Zither accompaniment

MR. FRANK BERTRAND, BARITONE
Queen of the Earth..Pensutti

MISSES ROSS AND HADLEY
Fancy Character Dancing Sketch...............
....Police Flirtation

Almost buried in the snow is the sign for the Nome Circulating Library at the Warwick. Most of the lodging houses in Nome operated lending libraries in the wintertime.
(Museum of History and Industry)

could shoot a powerful stream of water 90 feet in the air.[27] The Sisters of Charity operated a 50-bed hospital that was equipped with the latest in medical technology including "an improved X-Ray machine."[28]

The Nome Public Library had a collection that "would do credit to many a prosperous eastern city," of more than one thousand books and magazines. The library also had a full set of *Chambers Encyclopedia* for reference. A reader paid one dollar a month for the privilege of checking out any book for two weeks, and he could while away the long winter hours in the "warm and comfortable" reading room of the Congregational Church.[29]

One of the most unique signs of progress in Nome was the planking of the main streets and sidewalks. After 1901, pedestrians no longer had to wade through knee-deep mud on Front Street in hip boots. At a cost of thousands of dollars, most of the major business streets in Nome were paved with boards about 3 inches thick and 12 inches wide. The boards were laid across the street on about a half-dozen stringers. The sidewalks were also paved with wood and were usually about 8 feet wide, and slightly raised above street level. The street planking had to be constantly maintained and replaced, as the pavement rotted away quickly, and was soon worn out by the wagons and horses that rattled over it. Pedestrians were supposed to be able to walk the wooden streets in safety. An ordinance passed by the city council in the summer of 1901 prohibited "fast driving and riding" of wagons, horses, or bicycles, "at any such rate or speed as shall interfere with the reasonable use of the streets of the City of Nome by foot passengers."[30]

By 1905 the pedestrians were fighting for space on Nome's wooden streets with the first car in the city, a seven-passenger Thomas Flyer. The Alaska Automobile Transportation Company intended to use the car to haul passengers from Nome to Solomon on a private toll road. Though the project was never completed, a portion of the road was built between Nome and Fort Davis, and was probably the first "automobile road" in Alaska. The two-

This hand-cranked Thomas Flyer, with leather pouches on the doors, was one of the first automobiles in Nome. Sitting in the front passenger's seat is General A.W. Greely, the famous arctic explorer. (University of Washington Library, reprinted from *ALASKA GEOGRAPHIC®*)

mile stretch of gravel was a rugged highway, but the *Nome News* boasted that it "leaves many thoroughfares in the states away behind."[31]

The most important bridge in Nome was not built for automobiles. It was a $19,000 wooden drawbridge across the Snake River that William Geiger, a member of Nome's first city council, had constructed as a toll bridge during the 1900 stampede. The bridge was necessary to cross from the sand spit west of the Snake River to downtown Nome, but Geiger reduced his toll from 25¢ for each pedestrian to 5¢, when a man in a rowboat went into competition with him and started a ferry service at the cheaper rate.[32] Geiger made a fortune from the bridge before he sold it in 1902. The new owners were not as liberal as Geiger had been, however, and demanded that women and children also pay the toll. This made the people who lived on the sand spit east of the Snake River so angry that they planned to build a new drawbridge, but the city of Nome eventually purchased the bridge and abolished the toll.[33]

Several banks in Nome purchased gold dust from the mines. The Miners and Merchants Bank founded in 1904,

Geiger's toll drawbridge across the Snake River. The bridge was raised and lowered by hand with a system of weights and pulleys. (Paul Mogensen and Mark Hufstetler)

Paul Mogensen and Mark Hufstetler

Above — *In the early days Nome's main roads became rivers of mud when it rained.* **Right** — *A vast improvement came in 1905 when the first graveled "automobile road" in Alaska, here traveled by a man with a horse and wagon, was built from Nome to Fort Davis.*

bought $2 million worth of gold dust in its first year of operation, and melted down the dust into bars.[34] For many years the Miners and Merchants was the only bank in Nome, and the leading financial institution in northwestern Alaska. It was sold to the Alaska National Bank of Fairbanks in 1956.[35] One business with an even longer history in Nome was a newspaper founded in 1901 that is still in operation today, the *Nome Nugget.*

Nome was a good newspaper town. The *Nome Nugget* was one of more than a half-dozen daily or weekly newspapers once published in the city including the *Arctic Weekly Sun,* the *Nome Chronicle,* the *Nome Gold Digger* (known to rival papers as the "Nome Grave Digger"), the *Nome News,* and the *Nome Pioneer Press.* Of them all only the *Nome Nugget* survived after 1910.

Ethel Becker

Arwine Company

114

CHILDREN

The children of Nome grew up in a town that was quite different from most communities. Yet like children everywhere, life for them was one discovery after another. **Upper left** — *A berry picking expedition on Anvil Creek.* **Lower left** — *Exercise time for the third and fourth grade.* **Upper right** — *A group of native children.* **Lower right** — *Swimming in the Bering Sea.* **Below** — *A few of Miss Staple's fourth grade students in 1904. The short boy wearing coveralls in the back row is Jimmy Doolittle, who led Doolittle's raid on Tokyo during World War II.*

Leta Hamilton

Arwine Company

Thomas McGinn Smith

115

J.F.A. Strong, the founder of the Nome Nugget. (Lomen Collection, University of Alaska Archives)

The greatest newspaperman in Nome's early years was probably John Franklin Alexander Strong. J.F.A. Strong was a wandering journalist who had put out newspapers in Skagway and Dawson City before moving on to found Nome's first newspaper in October 1899, the *Nome News.* In 1901 he purchased the *Nome Chronicle* and founded a paper called the *Nome Nugget,* which he ran until he left Nome five years later. Strong went on to found three more newspapers in Alaska, two of which soon disappeared along with the towns where he founded them, the *Katalla Herald* and the *Iditarod Nugget,* and one which is still published today, the *Juneau Empire.*

In his long career the newspaperman with four names angered politicians in every town from Skagway to Nome, and he eventually became one himself, serving as governor of Alaska from 1913 to 1918. He was fired from the job by President Wilson when it was discovered that he was not from Kentucky as he had always claimed, but was a Canadian citizen from New Brunswick and not eligible for the position. Even today not much is known about his shadowy past, but it was also alleged that the name J.F.A. Strong was an alias, and that he was a bigamist who had deserted his first wife and several children in New Brunswick.[36]

J.F.A. Strong's Nome newspaper has survived numerous floods, fires, and other disasters over the years. Its irregular publication history has mirrored both the good days and hard times on the Seward Peninsula. When the economy was prospering it was a daily newspaper, but during leaner periods it was sometimes a tri-weekly, a semi-weekly, or a weekly. After the *Nugget*'s plant was completely destroyed in the 1934 fire, it appeared on a mimeographed sheet for a month and a half, and during World War II the paper suspended publication completely for about a year. The *Nugget* resumed publication in 1943, and has been going strong ever since under a half-dozen different publishers. The last surviving gold rush newspaper in Nome boasts today on its flag that it is the oldest newspaper in Alaska, and is "Published Daily except for Monday, Tuesday, Wednesday, Friday, Saturday and Sunday."

Back in the days when the newspapers in Nome really were published on every day of the week, the Northwestern Commercial Company had plans to build a street railway system that could have encircled the city. Electric trolley cars never clanged around the streets of Nome, but the Northwestern Commercial Company did

NOME NUGGET

SATURDAY, JUNE 1, 1907

CORWIN EXTRA

CORWIN ARRIVED IN ROADSTEAD LAST TUESDAY EVENING

Louis Hanak was the first person to arrive in Nome off the Corwin. Following Mr. Hanak was W. B. McCarthy, H. F. Dohohue, J. G. Frost, C. W. Hoxsie, G. Triplet, Jno. Bagge, G. D. Swan.

The Corwin, Capt. West in command, arrived in the roadstead last Tuesday and has been beating her way through the ice about 60 miles out ever since.

A boat was seen plainly about 6 o'clock this evening and was recognized by A. Gibson at 6:30 as the Corwin.

Quite a number of passengers are now on their way in over the ice.

A number of dog teams have started out and are bringing in passengers and mail.

The above named passengers took 1 hour and 30 minutes to reach the Sandspit after leaving the Corwin.

Leta Hamilton

The arrival of the first ship of the season was one of the big news events of the year. When the Corwin *(above) reached Nome in 1907, the* Nome Nugget *broadcast the news with this one-page extra edition.*

build an "elevated railway" to haul freight from the docks to their warehouse facilities. The Northwestern's bridge across Second Avenue said on the side, "Look Out for the Cars."[37]

From its earliest days, however, Nome did have a railroad. In the summer of 1900 Charles D. Lane built a five-mile-long, narrow-gauge line from tidewater to Discovery Claim on Anvil Creek to haul freight and supplies to his mining claims. It was the first railway in northwestern Alaska and was called the Wild Goose Railroad.

Every morning shortly before seven o'clock the little locomotive gave a loud whistle and pulled away for the mines on Anvil Creek with six loaded flatcars in tow. Freight took precedence over passengers on the train, but a canvas top was added to one of the flatcars to protect the travelers from inclement weather.[38]

In later years the tiny narrow-gauge line was extended almost 90 miles north of Nome to Shelton on the Kuzitrin River. The line was in commercial operation until about 1910, when regular service was discontinued. For many years after the last scheduled train left Nome, local residents continued to operate an assortment of rigs on the railroad tracks. Wagons or trailers pulled by dogs (known as pupmobiles) were a common sight along the tracks, as were automobiles, jeeps, and trucks with flanged wheels.[39]

Nome also had a baseball park. The national pastime had long been popular in Nome, and a series of games had been played in the city as early as the winter of 1900, when a team of soldiers battled a squad from the Alaska Commercial Company in mid-February. One game was called off after four innings "on account of the icy breezes from the north, [which made] it decidedly uncomfortable for the boys." It was so uncomfortable that the pitcher for the Alaska Commercial Company, Louis L. Lane, froze his fingers, and the contest was postponed until the arrival of milder weather.[40]

In the summer of 1908 the Nome Baseball Association was formed to promote baseball in Nome and to build a "first class diamond and field."[41] It was headed by J.C. Gaffney, the owner of a Nome clothing store, and other businessmen in the city who enjoyed playing and

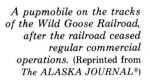

A pupmobile on the tracks of the Wild Goose Railroad, after the railroad ceased regular commercial operations. (Reprinted from *The ALASKA JOURNAL®*)

watching the grand old game. They built a ball park to the north of the city, by scraping away the vegetation and covering the tundra with a layer of burlap bags. On top of the jute sacks they spread out sand and gravel, and covered this layer with four inches of dirt. It was probably the most unusual baseball field in the world. "The grounds were a surprise to many," one newspaperman wrote, "as it was not believed that such a good infield could be made in this country."[42]

The park's grandstand had room for about five hundred people, and the bleachers held another four hundred, but the standing-room-only crowd at the first game of the 1908 season was estimated at nearly fifteen hundred, and they watched the Nome Red Socks beat the Federal Labor Union team by a score of 5 to 3. "The Reds looked very nifty in their white uniforms and red stockings," one reporter wrote, "while the Union men also put up a fine appearance in their neat and business like suits of gray."[43]

The city with the baseball diamond on the tundra was hardly a typical American town. The population of the city had stabilized somewhat after the gold rush, but every summer a small-scale reenactment of the 1900 landing on the Nome beach took place, as the first ships of the season raced each other into the roadstead and unloaded the miners, professional men, families and tourists who had spent the winter on the outside and were coming north for the summer.

Photo by F.H. Nowell   6000 Tons Coal — 108000 Sacks of the JOHN J. SESNON Co. Nome, Alaska, Aug. 1st 1905   4064

The town of Nome was icebound for seven months or longer each year, and there was always a rush to catch the last southbound ships in the fall.
(Ethel Becker)

People sometimes claimed that the only seasons in Nome were winter and the Fourth of July. It was not quite that bad, though the winters were seven months long, and the real summer mining season only lasted about one hundred days. In few other towns in the world were the contrasts between the summer and winter as stark, and the city was a far different place in January than it was in June. During the seven months of the closed season from November to May, the town was cut off from the rest of the world like a colony of Robinson Crusoes.

Every fall the city of Nome prepared itself as best it could for the long months of winter isolation. Along with the annual exodus of Nome's thousands of summertime residents every October, the authorities deported or blue- ticketed to Seattle any "undesirable characters," in- cluding vagrants, known criminals, and those without visible means of income, on one of the last boats leaving Nome in the fall. The thinking was that a vagrant had a better chance of surviving the winter in Seattle, rather than in Nome, and the Nome police were only too glad to send their problem cases to the Seattle police department.

Huge quantities of food and other supplies were stock- piled to feed the city during the seven months of winter. During the summer of 1905, for example, the Pacific Cold Storage Company shipped 1,000 sheep, 300 head of beef cattle, and 150 hogs to Nome, and slaughtered them. Over a typical winter they stored about 250 tons of stall fed meat for winter consumption.[44]

Supplies for the winter: 108,000 bags of coal, and a dozen barrels of Olympia beer. (Bancroft Library)

Just as important as stocking up on preserved meats or canned goods was accepting the fact that once the Nome fleet sailed south for the last time in October, it would not come again with fresh food, news of the outside world, or old friends, until the following June or July.

"We are prisoners in a jail of ice and snow," one Nome newspaperman wrote in late November 1900. He did not look forward to the coming winter. "The last boats may be justifiably considered to have gone and this little community of 4,000 to 6,000 people is left to its own resources, alone with the storms, alone with the darkness and chill of the North."[45]

During the winter of 1900-1901 the people of Nome had no telegraphic or wireless communication with the outside world, and it took three to four months for the mail carriers to reach Nome by dog team after freezeup. One of the big mysteries in Nome that winter was: Who was the president of the United States?

The 1900 election had been held on November 6, 1900, and for months afterward no one in Nome knew whether William McKinley had been elected to a second term, or if the Democratic challenger, the silver-tongued William Jennings Bryan, had defeated him. The people of Nome held their own election at the Nome Circulating Library, which Bryan won in a landslide with 520 votes compared to only 325 for McKinley, and 1 vote for the Socialist candidate, Eugene Debs.[46]

As the weeks passed curiosity built up over the identity of the next president, and many wagers were laid on the outcome of the nationwide election. The *Nome Gold Digger* sponsored a presidential guessing contest and announced in mid-November that a gold watch charm and cuff links would be given to the man and woman whose guesses were closest to the mark.[47]

The most optimistic forecasters had hoped that word of the winner would arrive in Nome by mid-December, but Christmas and New Year's came and went without any news. Finally on February 5, 1901, one day short of three months after the election, Nome was the last city in America to learn that McKinley had defeated Bryan for the second time.

The newspapers in Nome each tried to scoop each other with the three-month-old election news, the source of which was a month-old copy of a small newspaper from Rampart that the mail carriers had brought with them. The *Nome Chronicle* was the first on the streets with an extra at ten o'clock Tuesday night, "over an hour before any other paper was out." The *Nome News* also claimed to have reported the election results first. The *Chronicle* said that the *News* was lying, and that their breaking the news of McKinley's reelection before the *News* was the "most decisive 'scoop'" ever pulled off by a newspaper in Alaska.[48]

Though the residents of Nome were completely cut off from the outside world, editor Strong of the *Nome Nugget* said that no one should feel sorry for them. Because they lived at the end of the world the people of Nome, he thought, "could see what a farce and humbug this modern alleged civilization is."[49] Yet Strong regularly warned his readers about the tendency of people left alone to become hermits, and the other "evils of isolation."

Perhaps because Nome was so far away from everywhere else, it was one of the most sociable towns imaginable during the wintertime. When the snow piled deep against the doorways of the main businesses downtown and drifts nearly as high as the second-story windows clogged Front Street, the people of Nome had a wide variety of parties, social activities, and other entertainment to choose from. Saloons did a brisk business, and pool and billiard tournaments were popular. Numerous clubs and other societies, including the Saturday Evening Social Club, the 20th Century Club, church affiliated guilds and societies, and even a social chapter of the Ku Klux Klan, held their gatherings. The 15-piece Nome Philharmonic Orchestra under the direction of Professor Dugan, provided musical entertainment. "Few cities with a population of 25,000 and renowned

On February 5, 1901, three months after the 1900 election, Nome was about the last city in America to learn that William McKinley had been elected for the second time.
(University of Washington Library)

The Peoples Paper

THE NOME CHRONICLE

The Miners Friend

WE LEAD, OTHERS FOLLOW.

VOL. 1. NO. 20. NOME, ALASKA, TUESDAY, FEBRUARY 5, 1901. PRICE 25 CENTS.

EXTRA

McKinley Re-Elected

MAIL CARRIERS JUST ARRIVED WITH THE PRESIDENTIAL ELECTION NEWS.

HURRAH FOR McKINLEY

McKinley is re-elected with a bigger majority than in 1896. The full report of the votes by States is given in the following, taken from the Rampart Forum of January 3rd, and is substantiated by many personal letters from Dawson and Eagle.

The news created intense sensation in Nome. Just before the Chronicle's first extra, announcing the result, many were the bets offered on either side and it only needed the Chronicle's word to precipitate the greatest excitement that has ever been seen in this city.

This is what the Forum says:

Washington, Nov. 12—McKinley and Roosevelt have swept the electoral college but it looks as if Bryan will have the popular vote.

McKinley was elected by a larger majority than he had in 1896.

Full Account of the Election Given Here---With the Votes by States.

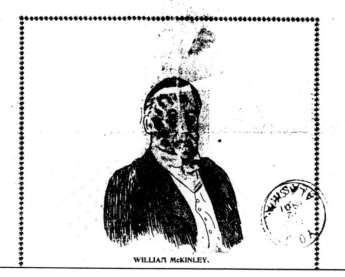

WILLIAM McKINLEY.

Election Vote for President in 1896.

Following is the electoral vote for McKinley and Bryan in 1896, by States:

States	Bryan	McKinley
.....	11	
Arkansas	8	
California	1	8
Colorado	4	
Connecticut		6
Delaware		3
Florida	4	
Georgia	13	
Idaho	3	
Illinois		24
Indiana		15
Iowa		13
Kansas	10	
Kentucky	1	12
Louisiana	8	
Maine		6
Maryland		8
Massachusetts		15
Michigan		14
Minnesota		9
Mississippi	9	
Missouri	17	
Montana	3	
Nebraska	8	
Nevada	3	
New Hampshire		4
New Jersey		10
New York		36
North Carolina	11	
North Dakota		3
Ohio	23	
Oregon		4
Pennsylvania		32
Rhode Island		4

"THE LIGHTNING STRIKERS"

WINNERS OF THE LADIE'S INDOOR BASEBALL LEAGUE TROPHY, NOME ALASKA, 1914

LOMEN BROS. NOME

Anchorage Historical and Fine Arts Museum

WINTER SPORTS

*D*og racing was the most famous wintertime sport in Nome, but there were others. **Top right** — Skiing and sledding on Dry Creek. **Lower right** — Ice-skating on the Snake River. **Below** — A popular sport was indoor baseball, a game much like modern-day softball played indoors. One of the best players on the Eagles team, jeweler Harry Hagen, middle row on the right, was the coach (left) of The Lightning Strikers, the ladies' championship indoor baseball team in 1914.

Seppala Collection, University of Alaska Archives

Museum of History and Industry

Bancroft Library

125

The Arctic Brotherhood Basketball team was the perennial roundball champion in Nome. (Reprinted from *The ALASKA JOURNAL®*)

balcony stretched up to near the top of the high ceiling, and spectators could see works by Gilbert and Sullivan, or watch a 50-mile marathon race, or a game of indoor baseball, a popular sport at the turn of the century somewhat like modern-day softball played indoors.

The most popular indoor sport was basketball, and during the winter the games at the Arctic Brotherhood gym or the Eagles Hall every Friday night were the social events of the week. Besides the A.B.'s and the Eagles, the Nome High School, the YMCA, and the soldiers from Fort Davis all established teams. They competed each year for the Shaw-Brewster Trophies, which were awarded to the best indoor baseball and basketball teams in the city. The seven-game playoffs for the trophies were the highlight of the season, and thousands of dollars were wagered on the outcomes. The basketball games were low-scoring affairs, as judged by modern standards, but no less exciting. Fans brought whistles and horns, but these were eventually outlawed in deference to the ladies, and because new players to the game were sometimes fooled and stopped playing when fans of the opposing team blew whistles and shouted "foul."[52]

Basketball was a new game, and it was a perfect sport for a place like Nome. At the time the Nome boys were as good as any players in the country. In 1907 the Arctic Brotherhood sponsored a Nome team that toured the United States hoping to become the "national champions." They played nearly 80 games against teams all across the country from California to New York, and the Nome squad only lost about a dozen times.[53]

Not all the winter sports activities were indoors. Ice skating was a favorite pastime of many Nome residents at the rink on the ice of the Snake River. The rink was enclosed from the weather by a 50-by-150-foot tent, and was surrounded by a wooden wall 3 feet high.

Those who enjoyed shooting could join the Nome gun club, which was equipped with 15,000 clay pigeons at which the members could merrily blaze away during its first winter season in 1902. The Nome Ski Club was an

as musical centers can boast of a finer organization," wrote the *Nome Nugget* about the local band.[50] Those with a literary bent could join the Nome Literary and Debating Society, and discuss the pros and cons of issues such as capital punishment, the role of the worker in modern society, or should the U.S. keep the Philippines.

The most active organizations of all were probably the fraternal societies such as the Eagles, the Arctic Brotherhood, and the Pioneers of Alaska. They not only sponsored dances and other social affairs, but also a wide variety of sports events. The Eagles Hall, built in 1906, was the largest building in Nome, and so dominated the skyline of the city that it reportedly could be seen from Sledge Island 25 miles away. The hall was a combination gymnasium, theater, and social hall.[51] A three-tiered active organization and built a ski slide that was 35 feet high, as well as a toboggan run on Dry Creek outside of Nome. All men in Nome of "good moral standing" were eligible to join and to participate in what was called the manly sport of skiing. A few women in Nome skied in their long ankle-length dresses and were permitted to become honorary members of the club.[54]

Three of the best skiers in Nome were the Seppala brothers, Leonhard, Asle, and Sigurd. It was not for his prowess on skis, however, that Leonhard Seppala is remembered today, for he was one of the greatest sled dog racers who ever lived.

Nome relied more on dog teams and the skill of the men who drove them than probably any other city in Alaska. All long-distance winter travel to Nome was usually by dog team, and mail carriers and others sometimes mushed thousands of miles every year. As Frank Dufresne, an Alaskan outdoorsman who mushed 17,000 miles in his career, once said, "All dog trails lead to Nome."[55]

With the best dogs and the best dog drivers in the country, Nome before World War I was the dog racing capital of the world, and the All-Alaska Sweepstakes was to Nome as the Kentucky Derby is to Louisville. This annual 408-mile race from Nome to Candle and back was thought by many to be the most grueling test of endurance and speed ever run in any sport. It was held every spring from 1908 to 1917, and was the most exciting event of the year. The teams left one minute apart from downtown Nome, and Front Street was jammed with spectators trying to get a glimpse of the dogs at the starting line. Headquarters for the race was the Board of Trade Saloon, where telephone reports, received of the racers' progress throughout the race, were recorded on a huge blackboard, as the eager crowds cheered and gambled more money than they should have on their favorites like Scotty Allan, Iron Man Johnson, or Leonhard Seppala.

The All-Alaska Sweepstakes was held for the last time

Leonhard Seppala and some of his trophies. Seppala was one of the greatest dog mushers who ever lived. (Lomen Collection, University of Alaska Archives.)

Scorecard of the last running of the All-Alaska Sweepstakes in 1917, which was won by Leonhard Seppala. (Glenbow Archives)

in 1917, the year that America entered World War I. Throughout Alaska, both population and gold production plummeted during the war, and Nome was even more depressed than most Alaskan cities. Gold production had been declining on the Seward Peninsula for a decade, but the downward spiral really started with the great storm of 1913, which nearly destroyed the city.

Since the first big storm hit Nome in September 1900, the city has been pounded regularly over the years by the wind and the waves. One of the most destructive storms of all, however, was in early October 1913 when it must have seemed to the people of Nome that the end of the world had come.

For several days the storm blew, and the water rose higher and higher. The ocean waves broke over the top of the city, smashing at first glass windows, and then

The start of the Solomon Derby from downtown Nome, March 2, 1914. (Anchorage Historical and Fine Arts Museum)

NOME, ALASKA, MARCH 2, 1914 — MCLEAN DARLING ENTRY, PERCY BLATCHFORD, DRIVER

WAVES WASHING HOUSES OFF SANDSPIT DURING STORM 1902 NOME

321.a.
W&S

Ethel Becker

STORMS

*B*ecause of its exposed location on the shore of the Bering Sea, every storm that blows across Norton Sound hits the city of Nome with full force.
Left — Waves washing houses off the Nome sand spit in 1902. **Top right** — To keep buildings from washing away in a storm, they often had to be tied down, as was the house in the foreground. **Lower right** — Breakers crashing down on an office building. **Below** — The wreck of the Harriet on the Nome beach in 1900.

Ethel Becker

Ethel Becker

Ethel Becker

131

The 1913 storm tore buildings off their foundations and smashed others to pieces (above and right). (Both photos by Carl B. Lancaster)

entire business blocks. Many buildings on Front Street were picked up off their foundations and hurled by the waves across the street to smash into other structures, as the "debris from broken and destroyed buildings crashed into the streets again on the angry summits of the rollers."[56] When the storm finally subsided, a *Nugget* reporter thought that Nome looked like it had been "shelled by a hostile fleet."

The east end of the city and central business district along the waterfront were destroyed. "Coming west one finds the Sesnon wharf demolished and the electric light plant flooded," the *Nugget* reported on October 8, 1913. "From there along the south side of Front Street the fine store buildings are only the gaping corpses of what they were. The backs of the buildings are torn out completely and nothing is left but the gaping fronts through which the sea tore Sunday and Monday morning into the street leaving nothing but the skeletons."

The houses and the street on the sand spit had completely disappeared, as had the native village on the spit and the Snake River bridge. The sand spit graveyard was also wrecked. "The graves were torn up and scores of coffins can be seen," the *Nugget* stated, "jutting out from the face of the tundra. Corpses were torn from the coffins and are now scattered along Snake River amid the flotsam and jetsam of the storm."

The washing out of the graveyard gave rise to one of the most famous legends in Nome, of which there are several versions. A surprised miner supposedly had to bury his wife, or a beautiful dance hall girl, for the second time, after her body, perfectly preserved, was uncovered by the 1913 storm and came floating back from the grave.

Many of the survivors of the 1913 storm left Nome and didn't come back. Afterward the city was never the same again.

After the 1913 storm it was said that Nome looked like it had been "shelled by a hostile fleet." (Carrie McLain Museum)

*Nome in the wintertime looking east across the Snake River. In the
distance on the left is the lighted cross on the steeple of Saint
Joseph's Catholic Church.* (Lulu Fairbanks Collection,
University of Alaska Archives.)

Chapter VII
The Hardest Years

The city of Nome was almost wiped out during World War I, but not by guns or bullets or poison gas. The gold mining industry throughout Alaska collapsed during the war, and in Nome gold production declined by more than two-thirds between 1916 and 1918. Many Alaskans left the territory to enlist in the army or to take high-paying wartime jobs then available in the states. Only 852 people were left in Nome by the time of the 1920 census.

The worst scourge of the war to touch Nome was the worldwide epidemic of Spanish influenza that killed about 20 million people in Africa, Asia, Europe, and America in 1918-19. Perhaps the people of Nome thought they were far enough away to be spared from the dreaded disease, as no cases were reported until October 1918, when the old steamship *Victoria* arrived in the Nome roadstead. The 48-year-old, iron-hulled *Vic* was one of the largest and most reliable vessels in the Nome fleet. On her last trip to Nome during the season of 1918, however, the *Vic* became a death ship, and she carried the deadly influenza germs north with her.

The *Victoria* was quarantined and fumigated when she landed at Nome, but the rules could not be strictly enforced. "To prohibit the landing of freight and supplies on which Nome and the north depended entirely for the fast approaching winter," one government official explained later, "would be to bring about a famine and probably precipitate a riot. . . ."[1]

Within a few days of the arrival of the *Victoria* the disease started to spread in the city of Nome, though at first no one realized the serious nature of the illness. It was thought to be the usual grippe that spread through the community every fall. In a matter of weeks, however, it became apparent that this disease was no ordinary fall cold.

"As the toll of deaths grew," E.D. Evans, the acting superintendent of the Bureau of Education wrote, "a silent horror fell on the people for it seemed as though the whole country was doomed; as one walked through the streets of Nome it seemed a city of the dead."[2]

Few people were left in Nome anyway. When the *Victoria* sailed south on October 28, 1918, with more than 700 passengers on board, it was estimated that only 500 to 600 people remained behind in Nome for the winter. The passengers who had jammed the overcrowded *Victoria* were not spared either, as the influenza appeared on board the ship shortly after it left Nome, and the trip to Seattle became the *Vic*'s famous race with death. Battling winter storms and waves that broke over the bow of the ship, the *Victoria* steamed full speed to the south. By the time she reached Seattle 153 of her panic-stricken passengers had caught the flu, and 4 were already dead, though only one of the fatalities on the ship was directly caused by the flu. When it docked in Seattle the *Victoria* was met by 17 ambulances at the wharf, which rushed more than 100 of the sick passengers to the emergency flu hospital.[3]

The disease was far more deadly for those left behind in Nome, where about 90 percent of the population caught the disease. Only about 30 whites died, but the death toll among the Eskimo people was staggering. "From ten to twenty natives were dying each day on an average in Nome," acting education superintendent Evans wrote, "and the dead wagon was in use constantly, going round to hunt for them and remove them."[4] Many of the sick froze to death, and their bodies were stacked in the

S.S. "VICTORIA"

hearse like cordwood. Across the Seward Peninsula the story was the same, with entire Eskimo families found dead in their shelters, and their bodies occasionally eaten by dogs. In 1918 the Eskimo population in the Nome region was estimated to be about 250, and of those, 200 died. Across northwestern Alaska more than 700 people perished that winter from the flu, a figure only slightly less than the total population of the city of Nome.[5]

The tragedy of the Spanish flu epidemic and the continual decline of the gold mining industry seemed to mark the city of Nome for extinction. In the early twenties the *San Francisco Chronicle* published an obituary for the city, and predicted that Nome would soon be deserted. "The thousands that around the beginning of the century made Nome a city are gone, dead or scattered to the ends of the earth," the *Chronicle* stated, "and none have come to take their place." The abandoned buildings would be burned "to warm the few human beings who cling to that desolate beach," and soon passing sailors would argue about where the city had once stood, as if it had been the site of an ancient, forgotten civilization.[6]

The irony was that the *Chronicle* blamed the gold dredging machines, which worked large amounts of mining ground with little labor, as the major cause of Nome's eventual death. In the long run however, the dredges were a main reason why the city managed to survive.

Gold dredges had been common in Nome since the beginning of the gold rush, but the later machines were far more practical than the 1900 monsters which had been built to mine the Nome beach. After 1908 mine operators began to construct more gold dredges on the Seward Peninsula every year, and the huge machines eventually replaced the hundreds of miners who had worked with a pick and shovel. By 1912 it was estimated that 25 percent of all the dredges in the United States were on the Seward Peninsula.[7] Of the 33 operating dredges on the Seward Peninsula that year, 10 of them were in the Nome region.

136

The SS Victoria *carried the deadly influenza germs north on her last trip in 1918.* (Powell Collection, University of Alaska Archives)

Hydraulic miners on Glacier Creek outside of Nome in 1910,
stripping away the overburden with high-pressure streams of water.
(Powell Collection, University of Alaska Archives)

Most of the early gold dredges were unsuccessful due to the inexperience of the operators, who often built them in areas that were not rich enough to be mined profitably. The early dredge owners did not have an inexpensive way of thawing huge blocks of frozen ground, and only in the few areas where the ground was not frozen could the dredges operate profitably.

A new era in the history of mining on the Seward Peninsula began in the early 1920s, when the Hammon Consolidated Gold Company purchased all the property of the Pioneer Mining Company, the firm that had been established by the three lucky Swedes in the early days of the camp. Jafet Lindeberg claimed that during the 23 years he was in Nome, his company averaged about a million dollars a year, making a huge fortune for all three of the founders of Nome. Little is known about John Brynteson, though apparently he returned to Sweden and lived in Stockholm.[8] Eric Lindblom never again had to sew others men's suits. The little tailor enjoyed the high life wearing fancy clothes and driving expensive automobiles, thanks to the day that he got lucky in 1898. He was also the founder of the Swedish-American bank of San Francisco, the owner of the Parral Electric Water and Telephone Company in Parral, Mexico, and the builder of the famous Claremont Hotel for millionaires in California. Lindblom died in 1928.[9] Jafet Lindeberg outlived Lindblom by almost 40 years. He died in 1962 at the age of 88 after a long career as a financier and investor, building upon the fortune that he had made in Nome. Many pioneer Alaskans hated him for as long as he lived, however, because Lindeberg's Scandinavian-American Bank of Tacoma failed about the same time that he sold his interests in the Pioneer Mining Company in the early 1920s. Many of those who had trusted him lost their life savings.[10]

The passing of the old Pioneer Mining Company in the early 1920s marked a shift from hydraulic mining to dredging. When the Hammon Consolidated Gold Company bought out the Pioneer Mining Company, the new

To supply the millions of gallons of water needed for hydraulic operations, miners dug miles of ditches on the Seward Peninsula.
(Ethel Becker)

firm hoped to mine the ground more efficiently with several huge electric-powered dredges, in ground thawed by cold water.

One of the major expenses faced by early-day miners and dredge operators in Alaska was the prohibitive cost of thawing frozen ground, which greatly limited the area that could be mined or dredged. Heating water to thaw the frozen ground was so expensive that only small areas of the very richest ground could be profitably mined. This expense was greatly reduced when the remarkable discovery was made that cold river water could thaw permanently frozen ground in the subarctic as effectively as hot water or steam.

The development of the cold water thawing method was a turning point in the history of the region because it opened the door for large-scale dredges on the Seward

Thawing frozen ground with a bank of hot water pipes.

Peninsula. Mining companies could thaw frozen ground that had once been considered impractical to mine, and dredge the gold from it. Though it was not absolutely certain that cold water thawing would work on a large scale until 1925, Hammon Consolidated launched its first two dredges at Nome two years earlier on June 1, 1923. The mayor of Nome declared a public holiday, and most of the residents of the city attended the ceremony. Both of the huge mining machines had manganese steel buckets, and one of them could dig as deep as 60 feet below the surface.

The dredges were combination floating steam shovels and sluicing plants, powered by electricity from a diesel generator. As the steel scoops on the bucket line ate through the rocks they made an awful sound. Inside each dredge the huge quantities of gravel were washed and sifted along an assembly line of screens, separators, and conveyor belts. The gold was saved and the rest of the gravel was thrown out the back of the dredge by a long tailings stacker. When the machines were in operation they worked around the clock, but they were shut down about every 10 days or 2 weeks for the clean up of the gold. During the course of a 24-hour day one dredge, manned at all times by a crew of 12 to 14 men, could dig through approximately six thousand cubic yards of gold-bearing gravel.

One dredge did the work of hundreds of men, and could generally operate profitably in an area that had been rich enough for drift mining, by digging up entire river valleys and recovering the waste gold that early-day pick and shovel men had missed. Before a valley could be dredged however, the ground had to be thawed. Workers hammered hundreds of steel pipes known as points into the frozen gravel which were connected to a central water main. The mass of hoses and pipes across the ground that was being thawed was said to look something like a corn field. It was known as a point field. As the cold water slowly seeped into the gravel, workers hammered the points deeper and deeper, and the frozen ground grad-

ually melted around the steel pipes in ever widening circles.[11]

In the mid-twenties Hammon Consolidated was bought out by one of the largest mining corporations in the country, the United States Smelting, Refining and Mining Company, though the company was still known locally as Hammon Consolidated. The U.S.S.R.&M. Co. perfected the techniques of cold water thawing in 1925, and a year later, for the first time since before World War I, gold production in the Nome district totaled more than $1 million a year.[12] The U.S.S.R.&M. Co. continued to mine the golden gravels of the Nome district until 1962, when the dredges shut down. Usually the company operated two or three dredges every season and employed hundreds of laborers, except during World War II when the United States government classified gold mining as a non-essential industry and closed it down.[13]

In 1925, the same year that the U.S.S.R.&M. Co. perfected the cold water thawing method, which opened the district to gold dredging and provided Nome with an economic basis for almost 40 years, the city was almost devastated by a disease that could have been as deadly as the influenza epidemic of 1918. Diphtheria had broken out in the city. Enough antitoxin was available for only a few inoculations, but even that was five years old. The relay race by dog sled to rush fresh diphtheria serum nearly seven hundred miles to Nome in the winter of 1925 became one of the most famous events in Alaskan history.

In mid-January 1925 a few Native children in Nome came down with sore throats. Several of them died, but Dr. Curtis Welch, the only physician in Nome, did not diagnose the disease as diphtheria until January 21. The city council immediately declared a quarantine, and school was canceled, as were all social activities.

"All children should be compelled to wash their faces and hands frequently during the day with some MILD SOAP such as Ivory soap," the *Nome Nugget* warned. "A STRONG soap is worse than no soap at all as it has

Driving points into the frozen ground, with a dredge in the background. (Lomen Collection, University of Alaska Archives)

A point field near Nome. Using cold water to thaw the ground made large-scale dredging economical in the Nome district.
(Lomen Collection, University of Alaska Archives)

141

A dredge under full steam on the Solomon River. (Lomen Collection, University of Alaska Archives)

a tendency to cause the face and hands to chap and crack and render them easily susceptible to the Diphtheria germ."[14] Children are especially vulnerable to diphtheria, and the *Nugget* urged all parents to act as quarantine officers, and to isolate their own children.

Ivory soap, however, would not cure diphtheria, and the people of Nome would face further tragedy unless more antitoxin could be obtained. Mayor George Maynard wired Alaska's congressional delegate, Dan Sutherland, the man who had been the first to land on the Nome beach during the stampede of 1900, to send one million units of diphtheria serum by train to Nenana, the nearest town to Nome on the Alaska Railroad. Two fast dog teams, one from Nenana and one from Nome, could meet each other halfway between the two cities "in order to get the antitoxin to Nome as speedily as possible."[15]

As the days passed the disease spread, and by the end of January there were 22 reported cases of diphtheria,

30 suspected cases, 50 contacts, and 5 deaths. Speed was a matter of life and death. Some thought was given to using an airplane to carry the serum to Nome, but that was regarded as impractical under winter conditions. The authorities decided to hire the fastest dog drivers on the Yukon to run the 674 miles between Nenana and Nome in relays. Each team would sprint about 30 to 50 miles from one roadhouse or village to the next, before handing over the 20-pound package of serum to the next driver.

With the temperature at 42° below zero, the first musher, Wild Bill Shannon, left Nenana carrying the precious package which was wrapped in fur robes to keep it from freezing on the evening of January 27, 1925. While he was on the trail the temperature dropped as low as 62° below. His dogs started to bleed at the lungs, but he reached Tolovana shortly before noon the next day, where he handed the serum over to the next driver.[16]

Seven days later Gunnar Kaasen, the last of 20 mushers, stumbled into Nome behind his dog team through a blizzard, carrying the three hundred thousand units of diphtheria antitoxin. The serum was frozen solid when Kaasen arrived in Nome, but fortunately it did not harm the antitoxin. The worst of the crisis was over, though the quarantine in Nome was not officially lifted until several weeks later.[17]

The Nome diphtheria serum run made headlines all across the country. Gunnar Kaasen, the musher who ran the last 53 miles of the race to Nome, became a national hero as did his lead dog Balto. Kaasen recieved a gift of $1,000 from the drug company which manufactured the serum, as well as offers to lecture about his experiences. He also got a Hollywood contract "from a motion picture man to exhibit himself and [his] famous dog team in the movies."[18] His dog Balto had more lasting glory. The Balto Memorial Commission presented a bronze statue of the dog hero to New York City, which was erected in Central Park in 1925, and is still today a favorite with children who visit the park and love to ride on Balto's back. Later the children of Cleveland, Ohio, donated more than $2,000 in pennies to purchase Balto and Kaasen's other dogs, and when Balto died years later his body was mounted and put on exhibit in the Cleveland Museum of Natural History.[19]

Not everyone in Nome thought that Kaasen was a hero, or that Balto deserved to be either bronzed in New York, or stuffed in Cleveland. It was generally thought that the whole affair had been greatly exaggerated, and that the epidemic had never been a serious threat. "Nome people laughed at the whole thing," nurse Gertrude Ferguson wrote in late 1926, "and said that most of the scare was good newspaper work."[20]

Those who believed that the danger of the diphtheria epidemic had been real argued that the serum run had been the effort of all 20 mushers and hundreds of dogs. Leonhard Seppala, one of the greatest dog mushers in history, was especially angered. Originally Seppala was to carry the serum all the way from Nulato to Nome by himself. When it was decided that it would be much faster

In honor of the Nome diphtheria run, a bronze statue of Balto the dog hero was erected in New York's Central Park.
(New York Public Library)

143

for the serum to be relayed from one driver to another, Seppala ran the longest stretch of any single musher, 93 miles between Shaktoolik and Golovin. He also mushed along the dangerous trail across the ice of Norton Sound.

Kaasen mushed a total of 53 miles from Bluff to Nome, but he was not supposed to have run the last leg of the race to Nome. There are various versions of the story why Kaasen did not stop in the blizzard to turn over the serum to his relief driver and dog team at Port Safety, about 20 miles outside of Nome. But the result was that he drove the last leg of the race against death himself, supposedly led onward through the driving storm by the unerring instinct of his champion lead dog Balto, and was proclaimed as the man who saved Nome. Seppala claimed that Kaasen drove on to Nome to grab the glory and publicity, and that instead of a poor lead dog like Balto, Seppala's fine leader Togo should have been enshrined in Central Park.

Despite the controversy in Nome over which man or dog should have gotten the most credit, across the United States all of the men and their dogs were acknowledged as heroes. "This will probably be the last Alaskan race of its kind," stated a U.S. Senate bill honoring the serum mushers, "and is a fitting finish to a long list of records made by heroic men and dogs of the Northland."[21]

The day of the dog team was coming to an end in the city that had once been the dog racing capital of the world. About four months after the serum mushers reached Nome, Noel Wien, one of Alaska's most respected bush pilots, made the first commercial flight from Fairbanks to Nome. The diphtheria serum run demonstrated to the world how isolated Nome was during the wintertime, and showed the value of the newly developing aviation industry to the people of Alaska. Beginning in 1925, the same year that Balto was bronzed in Central Park, the dog team started to give way to the airplane as the major means of long-distance travel in Alaska for freight, mail, and passengers. Bush pilots gradually replaced dog drivers as the gallant men who regularly battled the wilderness between Alaska towns and mining camps, and by the eve of World War II most of the old dog trails had been abandoned.

One of the first flights in Nome, and probably all of Alaska, was a balloon ascension by "Leonard, Prince of the Air," in September 1901. The ballon rose about two thousand feet in the air and drifted a mile out to sea. In front of a crowd of several thousand people stretched along the waterfront, the balloonist put on a show. "Leonard performed on the trapeze during his aerial flight," the *Nugget* reported, "and when he dropped he must have fallen a couple of hundred feet before his parachute opened. He got a cold bath, but a boat was near at hand and picked him up."[22]

Another early flight was made at Nome a few years later in 1905 by "Professor Nemo," a self-styled "world famous aeronaut," who rose above Nome in a balloon airship for the May carnival held that year. Professor Nemo was just one of several attractions at the carnival, including a "world champion ball dodger" who challenged anyone in Nome to try to hit him with a baseball, and a Hindu swami who could read palms and reveal past, present and future.[23]

Professor Henry Peterson, a Nome music teacher, was not as flamboyant as Professor Nemo or the Prince of the Air, but he was the man who really attempted to

Professor Henry Peterson and his flying machine, before it was taken out of the warehouse. (Tom and Larry Martin)

Peterson at the controls of the first airplane in Alaska, shortly before he attempted his first flight. (Tom and Larry Martin)

Peterson's Tingmayuk never got off the ground, but one photographer faked a picture showing the plane carrying a load of passengers on the Nome cableway. (Carrie McLain Museum)

initiate the air age in the north when he built the first airplane in Alaska at Nome in 1911. Peterson was an eccentric fellow, and most Nome residents were amused by the machine he built, which the Eskimos called *Tingmayuk,* meaning "The Bird." It was a five-hundred-pound, wooden biplane covered with muslin and strung with piano wire. Peterson's flying machine had a gasoline engine and a pusher propeller much like the Wright Brothers' first successful model, but his plane was especially adapted to Alaskan conditions and was probably the first ski plane in the world.

"A novelty about the machine," the *Nome Nugget* reported, "which will not be seen upon the crafts used elsewhere in the country, is the rudder or ski carriage upon which the biplane body rests and which will convey the air vessel and its occupant over the hardened snow. This feature is peculiar to Mr. Peterson's craft alone as in no other clime where airships are used is there heavy snow to contend with."[24]

On the evening of May 9, 1911, nearly twelve hundred people showed up near the wireless tower behind the city of Nome to watch the first airplane flight in Alaska. Tickets for the event cost one dollar a piece. Peterson carefully inspected his machine, and with the help of some volunteers he dragged the five-hundred-pound biplane to an open stretch of ground on the snow-covered tundra.

"When the machine was finally settled on firm snow," the *Nugget* wrote the next day, "Mr. Peterson without hesitation mounted the driver's seat, and ordered the propeller started." With the inventor at the throttle sitting at the front end of the plane, the little engine behind his seat made a loud racket that could be heard for blocks around, and he began his takeoff. "The machine proceeded to move along the ground at a slow speed," a reporter said, "and after it had progressed in this manner for a few feet, it came to a halt."[25]

Several attempts were made to get the airplane off the ground, and finally Peterson dragged it to the top of a nearby hill and tried to get a running start coming down the slope, but all efforts were unsuccessful. After about an hour of standing around in the soft snow, "the crowd dispersed leaving Aviator Peterson, his machine and admirers stranded on Peluk hill."[26] So ended the saga of Henry Peterson's flying machine, the first airplane in Alaska.

Nine more years passed before the first successful flying machines darkened the skies of Nome. In August 1920 four army biplanes, each with the head of a black wolf painted on the tail, landed at Fort Davis outside of Nome, after having flown all the way from New York City. The flight of the famous Black Wolf Squadron from New York to Nome and return was planned by Gen. Billy Mitchell, the father of the air force and a longtime advocate of air power, who had been stationed in Alaska with the Signal Corps during the gold rush. Mitchell always believed that Alaska's central location in the Arctic made it the most strategic place in the world for aviation, and his often quoted phrase was, "He who holds Alaska, holds the world." Only after the start of World War II and the tensions of the Cold War which followed it, were Mitchell's beliefs widely accepted, but the flight of the Black Wolf Squadron proved to the people of Nome in 1920 that aviation in Alaska was feasible.

Flying low under a heavy cloud cover, four olive-green biplanes appeared over the eastern horizon on the evening of August 23, 1920. Almost everyone in Nome rushed out to greet them. "In the air they greatly resemble giant hawks," one reporter thought, "and make a most amazing amount of noise in full flight."[27] After flying circles over the city the planes headed for the landing field at Fort Davis, outside of Nome.

"Practically everyone in the city watched the thrilling spectacle as the flyers turned and circled above the field before swooping downward to make their landing," the *Nome Nugget* stated, "and cheer after cheer went up from the throng as the planes came to a halt one after the other at intervals of four or five minutes."[28] The army fliers were complimentary about the Nome landing field which had been especially prepared for them on the sandy soil at Fort Davis. Next to the river bar on the Yukon where they had landed at Ruby, they thought the Nome field was the finest in Alaska.[29]

The first plane to be based in Nome was Charles A. Lajotte's ill-fated World War I Jenny, which he shipped to Alaska in 1923. Lajotte had barnstormed across the country like hundreds of other former military pilots, and he thrilled the people of Nome with the first stunt flying over the city in August 1923. As Lajotte soared through the air, his friend and wingwalker D. Compton moved from one wing to another and crawled underneath the plane hanging on to the wheels. Lajotte made several short flights over Nome, taking up people in the passenger seat for $15 each, who wanted "the thrills of viewing their city from above the house tops."[30] Unfortunately the landing field at the parade grounds on Fort Davis was so poor that after a few flights Lajotte could not even take off with a full tank of gas let alone a passenger. In September he tried to fly from Nome to Council, but he got lost in bad weather and made a crash landing.

"The engine in the plane worked like a clock while the fuel lasted," the *Nome Nugget* reported. He left his plane sitting upside down on the tundra in the vicinity of Council City. Nineteen days after he crashed Lajotte safely returned to Nome, proving once again the saying that early-day Alaskan bush pilots often did more walking than flying.[31]

Noel Wien was a pilot who usually did not make a practice of landing upside down on the tundra. He has been called the first true bush pilot, "the working flyer who pulled Alaska from the stone age to the age of wings, from transport by dog sled and boat to airplanes."[32] Wien

Many of the early-day pilots around Nome did more walking than flying. (Lomen Collection, University of Alaska Archives)

made the first commercial flight to Nome in 1925 in a five-passenger Fokker that had red upholstered seats and drapes on the windows. A year later the Alaska Road Commission built Nome's first real airfield with two runways at a cost of $2,500, and in 1927 the young pilot from Minnesota started the first regularly scheduled airline service in Alaska. His new company, Wien Alaska Airways, began a weekly flight from Nome to Fairbanks in 1927 and kept up the service all through the winter. Noel and his brother Ralph made their own skis for the airplane, and learned how to keep it running when the temperature dropped to 60° below zero.[33]

The old-timers in Nome used to say, "Even God leaves on the last boat!"[34] By the early 1930s, however, Nome was no longer the isolated island of humanity during the winter months that it once had been. An airplane trip to Fairbanks, even with a fuel stop at Ruby, only took about seven hours. "The airplane," as Alfred Lomen said in 1933, "has put Fairbanks just across the street from Nome."[35]

The airplane was especially valuable for the Lomen family, because at the same time that the aviation industry was beginning to emerge, it began to appear as though the Lomens' reindeer herds might become the mainstay of the economy of northwestern Alaska. Reindeer "cowboys" rode the range across the tundra in airplanes in the late 1920s spotting herds, when reindeer herding became second only to gold mining as the major industry on the Seward Peninsula.

The early history of Nome is intertwined with the story of the reindeer industry. Many of the first prospectors in the Nome district, including Jafet Lindeberg, originally came to Alaska as reindeer herders. Reindeer are a sort of domesticated caribou. They were first brought to Alaska from Siberia by pioneer missionary Sheldon Jackson in the 1890s, who hoped that the animals would provide the Eskimos with a reliable source of food, clothing, and transportation, as the natural game animals they had traditionally relied upon were killed off.

By 1914 it was estimated that there were nearly 60,000

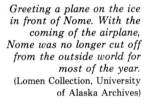

Greeting a plane on the ice in front of Nome. With the coming of the airplane, Nome was no longer cut off from the outside world for most of the year.
(Lomen Collection, University of Alaska Archives)

Top — *Noel Wien made the first commercial flight from Fairbanks to Nome in his Fokker F. III monoplane.* **Left and Above** — *Carl Ben Eielson's metal Hamilton loading at Nome.*

REINDEER

*T*he Lomen Company hoped to make their reindeer industry one of Alaska's most important. They envisioned herds of millions of reindeer grazing on the Seward Peninsula, with reindeer ranches that would rival the cattle ranges of Texas. They went to great lengths to promote reindeer meat. **Left** — A team of Lomen reindeer pulling Santa Claus's sleigh in a holiday parade. **Upper right** — The Lomens selling canned reindeer meat. **Lower right** — Reindeer carcasses for the Nome market, with a herd in the background on the Seward Peninsula. **Below** — A stock certificate for the Lomens' Alaska Livestock and Packing Company.

Lomen Collection, University of Alaska Archives

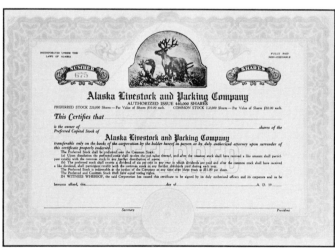

Lomen Collection, University of Alaska Archives

Denny Collection, University of Alaska Archives

The Lomen Company enlisted Santa Claus in their efforts to promote the reindeer industry. (Lomen Collection, University of Alaska Archives)

reindeer in Alaska. That same year Lomen and Company, backed in part by Jafet Lindeberg, became interested in the large-scale commercial possibilities of reindeer herding, which up to that time had been largely a subsistence activity for the Eskimos. They purchased a small herd of about 1,200 animals, and over the next 25 years the Lomen family came to dominate the reindeer business in northwestern Alaska.

The Lomen clan had deep roots in Nome. G.J. Lomen and his son Carl had come north from Minnesota during the great stampede of 1900. Later they were joined by Mrs. Lomen and the rest of the family including Carl's four brothers, Ralph, Harry, George, and Alfred. The family operated various businesses over the years, including a drugstore, a photo studio, merchandise stores, and a lighterage company, but the most unique Lomen enterprise was the reindeer corporation.[36]

Carl Lomen, the Reindeer King, spearheaded the business. He envisioned herds of millions of reindeer grazing on the tundra, with reindeer ranches on the Seward Peninsula that would rival the cattle ranges of Texas. The Lomens invested hundreds of thousands of

dollars in the enterprise, building corrals, slaughterhouses, cold storage plants, and refrigerated ships, and they planned to provide a hungry world that was becoming more populated every year with a new meat product raised in Alaska. Creating a market for reindeer meat proved to be as difficult as any facet of the industry, but the Lomens promoted their product all across the United States in several ingenious ways. They managed to have several railroads serve reindeer meat in their dining cars, outfitted arctic explorers and movie stars in reindeer clothing, and marketed reindeer dog food. They also supplied live reindeer to pull the sleighs of various Santa Clauses in the largest cities in the country.

The peak years of the reindeer industry were from 1927 to 1930, when the Lomens sold nearly 50,000 reindeer carcasses in four years, a total of about six million pounds of reindeer meat.[37] After 1930 the sales of reindeer meat plummeted. The Lomen reindeer industry collapsed during the Great Depression, but the nationwide economic disaster was not the only cause of the decline. Politically powerful cattlemen and sheep ranchers did their best to stop the introduction of reindeer meat in

The directors of the Lomen Company, including Jafet Lindeberg and G.J. Lomen second and third from the left, and Carl Lomen on the right. (Lomen Collection, University of Alaska Archives)

A 1901 parade down one of Nome's main business streets, Steadman Avenue. These narrow wooden streets doomed the gold rush city in the 1934 fire. (Ethel Becker)

the United States. Many people in Alaska opposed the Lomens, because it was felt that they were exploiting the Eskimos for whose benefit the reindeer had been introduced. In 1937 Congress passed the Alaska Reindeer Act, which directed the government to buy all the reindeer owned by non-Natives. By 1940 the Lomens had sold all of their herds, and their dream of a reindeer empire on the Seward Peninsula was a thing of the past.

After the 1930s the reindeer almost completely disappeared from northwestern Alaska. From a peak of more than a half-million in 1932, 20 years later the total reindeer population in Alaska had declined to about 27,000.[38] Many reasons have been given for the decline, including poor herding techniques, wolf predation, excessive slaughtering, and over grazing.[39]

During the 1920s and early 1930s the people of Nome hoped that the reindeer experiment would prove successful, and become another basic industry that would help bring prosperity back to the region. Travelers to Nome in those years always marveled at the number of abandoned buildings which lined the rotting wooden streets of the city, and remarked that the empty houses outnumbered inhabitants 10 to 1.[40]

"The whole town of Nome is a startling reminder of its former affluence," one traveler wrote in his diary in 1923. "Few of the houses and stores are occupied and with the exception of the houses of the members of the Lomen family, and their store, all are going to rack and ruin and many look as though they were about ready to fall with the next storm. The same applies to the board walks, the missing board and hole are the rule, not the exception."[41]

The many abandoned buildings in Nome made the town look like a "has been," a chamber of commerce publication admitted in the early 1930s, but they claimed that a more permanent city was slowly evolving even if the standing structures looked like they were all falling down. "Buildings which are occupied often give an impression of being poorly cared for," the chamber stated, "because of the fact that the ground on which Nome is built is frozen. The freezing and thawing tend to shift the buildings so that they need leveling every year or two. If this is not done the buildings often are leaning or twisted."[42]

The biggest hotel in Nome was the Golden Gate Hotel. The eminent anthropologist Ales Hrdlicka said the Golden Gate was so "badly out of plumb in several directions that one almost hesitates to walk by it."[43] Few outsiders were impressed by Nome's finest hotel. Frank Carpenter, one of the most famous travel writers in America, who was dubbed the Marco Polo of Sunday magazine writers, thought that the Golden Gate was nothing but a "dreary four story barn." The hotel charged $2.50 to $3.00 a night for a musty room in which it was impossible to sleep.

"The building is of light wood, which carries sound like a fiddle box," Carpenter wrote. "The moving of a bed on the ground floor sends a noise to rooms in the attic. The place is golden only in the high charges for any petty service the guest may want. It cost me ten cents to press the electric button which brings the bellboy, and the bills for laundry are beyond computation."[44] A later visitor found that the proprietor, who was also the porter, handyman, bellboy, and clerk, had torn out the call bells and the wires in each room, "saying that when any of

Front Street in Nome, before the 1934 fire.
(Beth Hunt)

155

A fashionable house in Nome.
(Anchorage Historical and Fine Arts Museum)

the guests wanted anything, they could get it themselves."[45]

The permanent residents of Nome could overlook such things. They were more likely to brag about Nome's Dream Theatre, the Farthest Northwest Sound Theater on the American Continent, which showed four talkie shows a week, shipping in enough films every fall to run all winter.[46] Though the houses in Nome may not have been particularly attractive by outside standards, they were warm and cozy. Many homes had pianos, Victrolas, and radios, the great craze of the 1920s. Radio reception in Nome was usually quite good during the winter, and during the long cold months radio buffs and those who wanted to keep up with the latest news from the outside world could pick up stations up and down the West Coast and as far away as Japan or Australia. Due to changes in the weather, however, sometimes nothing could be heard on the shortwave for weeks, leading one radio owner in Nome to comment, "There are two things in Alaska to teach a man to swear — a dog team and a radio."[47]

When Pres. Franklin D. Roosevelt was elected in 1932 the nation hoped he could lead the country out of the Great Depression. One of the earliest measures of the New Deal, and one of the most important as far as the people of Nome were concerned, was that FDR nearly doubled the price of gold to $35 an ounce in 1933. The future outlook for the mining industry in Nome and throughout Alaska brightened considerably. A small-scale gold boom took place and it was hoped that Nome was about to enjoy renewed prosperity. However, that was before the morning of September 17, 1934, when the worst fire in the history of Alaska struck the city of Nome.

It is not clear even today how the fire started. It is often said in Nome that a whiskey still blew up inside the Golden Gate Hotel.[48] Another story is that a group of homeless men were carousing around in an abandoned wing of the hotel and one carelessly tossed away a lighted

Ralph Lomen's telegram to his brother Carl, telling him about the 1934 holocaust. (Lomen Collection, University of Alaska Archives)

Charge to the account of _____ **Northwestern Livestock Corp.** $

CLASS OF SERVICE DESIRED

DOMESTIC	CABLE
TELEGRAM	FULL RATE
DAY LETTER	DEFERRED
NIGHT MESSAGE	NIGHT LETTER
NIGHT LETTER X	SHIP RADIOGRAM

Patrons should check class of service desired; otherwise message will be transmitted as a full-rate communication.

CHECK
ACCT'G INFMN.
TIME FILED

WESTERN UNION

R. B. WHITE
PRESIDENT

NEWCOMB CARLTON
CHAIRMAN OF THE BOARD

J. C. WILLEVER
FIRST VICE-PRESIDENT

Send the following message, subject to the terms on back hereof, which are hereby agreed to

September 18, 1934

Carl J. Lomen, 35 Fifth Ave.
New York, N. Y.

Fire started Golden Gate spread to include area Lincoln Hotel seven blocks west and three blocks north from beach stop reports state one hotel and Lomen Commercial saved all restaurants and grocery stocks except Polet warehouse at river destroyed stop all federal buildings total loss stop Lomen Brothers wiped out stop Tony Dimond in Alaska we suggest you proceed Washington endeavor have CC Camp enlisted from citizens Nome also endeavor ascertain what Federal aid can be secured stop prominent citizens Nome organizing for appeal Federal aid to rehabilitate city stop citizens being housed in warehouses and camp kitchens being established stop consult Admiral Hamlet stop press the immediate release remaining one forty seven and if possible conclusion other deal stop xxxxxxx no casualties reported except two eskimo Hospital out of zone caring for injured stop weather thirty eight wind moderated tonight stop Baldwin due Nome today south and Victoria twenty fourth north stop Jackson reports bank xxxxxxxxxxxx building total loss stop five loss estimated between two and three million stop immediate action imperitive to assemble supplies prior freeze up stop enlist Red Cross stop have been with AP and Wamcats all evening stop Nome station and Seattle maintaining continuous service tonight stop will keep you in close touch xxxp

Ralph Lomen.

The Golden Gate Hotel, on the left side of the street, burned down several times. It was the cause of Nome's first major fire in 1901, but was subsequently rebuilt. The doomed building caught fire again in 1934, and the fire destroyed most of downtown Nome.
(Bancroft Library)

cigarette butt.[49] It may have been a faulty wire, or a spark from a nearby chimney, but whatever the cause, the Golden Gate Hotel caught fire that morning in a 20- to 30-mile-an-hour wind, and by the time the blaze was under control about four hours later, most of what was left of gold rush Nome was gone.

The Golden Gate Hotel had burned down several times before, and had been the cause of Nome's first serious fire in 1901. The 1934 blaze that started in the doomed hotel was far more devastating than the earlier disasters. The fire began at about half past ten in the morning. Fanned by the strong east winds that may have gusted as high as 35 miles an hour, the fire quickly destroyed the hotel and spread to Front Street and downtown Nome. Unable to stop the blaze in the high winds, volunteers and fire fighters did their best to salvage anything they could carry out of the path of the wall of fire.

"When the fire began eating into the heart of the business district," a reporter wrote, "gravel trucks, livery wagons and private trucks and automobiles were commandeered to haul groceries and clothing a safe distance away. Men worked until they dropped in their tracks and were then helped away from the blazing and falling buildings by volunteer women."[50]

At the hardware store exploding rounds of ammunition sounded like machine gun fire, as one building after another started to burn. After several buildings were blown down with dynamite to make a fire break, the blaze stopped spreading, but not before all the wooden buildings, streets, and sidewalks for 12 city blocks were completely destroyed.

The next day a black cloud hung over the smoking ruins of the city of Nome. Total damage was estimated to be from $2 million to $3 million. Miraculously no one was reported killed in the fire, but gone were 65 businesses and 90 homes. Approximately two hundred people had lost everything, leaving one-fifth of the city's permanent population homeless. The immediate danger was the threat of starvation, because most of the coming winter's food supply had burned up in the fire.

Fresh supplies and building materials were immediately rushed to the stricken city. With winter fast approaching it was not certain if the community should try and rebuild immediately, or if the homeless should be evacuated for the winter.

Many chose to stay. With the assistance of the federal government, the Red Cross, and hundreds of local volunteers, the people of Nome started to build a new city on the ashes of the old one.[51]

For days after the fire, a black cloud hung over the smoking ruins of Nome. (Lomen Collection, University of Alaska Archives.)

159

Chapter VIII
A Town That Wouldn't Die

The limits of the great fire of 1934 are still visible today in Nome almost 50 years later. In downtown Nome, where the fire demolished everything, the streets are straight and broad as boulevards, especially Front Street. The city plat was redrawn in the burned district and the streets were widened in the aftermath of the disaster, so as to prevent another fire from destroying the city again. At the edge of the burned-out area however, the boulevards stop, and funnel into the narrow crooked back streets which were not touched in 1934.

Officials in Washington, D.C., had first proposed after the fire that Nome should be abandoned and the whole city moved to Teller, which has a deep-water harbor. It was not the last time that outsiders would suggest that Nome be moved to a more sheltered location. Instead Nome was rebuilt in the same place, in defiance of all the laws of nature and city planning.[1]

"The new Nome will rise as an example of what, in this day and age, is regarded as 20th century progress," a mimeographed edition of the *Nome Nugget* said after the fire destroyed its printing press. The gold rush was over, and the people of Nome were determined not to build a city that would be known for its "gambling halls and hard-bitten individuals."[2]

"Buildings to be constructed now will not be put up over-night as flimsy or as carelessly as before. Instead every effort is being made to regulate and restrict such antiquated methods of construction as were used in 1900. . . ."[3]

One major hope in the 1930s for the new Nome was that it might become an international aviation center because of its strategic location. Instead of an isolated, icebound seaport without a harbor, visionaries argued that Nome was the center of future world commercial and aviation routes.

The first trans-polar flight from the old world to the new was made in 1926 by explorer Roald Amundsen, in the dirigible *Norge*. Amundsen, who was a frequent visitor at Nome on his way to and from the arctic, had originally planned to end his flight at Nome, but was forced to land instead at Teller.

A year later the chamber of commerce installed large cables anchored in cement at Nome's aviation field for an airship anchorage, and for a time it appeared that Nome might be the base of operations for a series of polar flights to be made by the *Graf Zeppelin*, the predecessor of the *Hindenburg*.[4]

In 1931 Wiley Post and his navigator Harold Gatty made the first round-the-world airplane flight in history, and stopped en route near Nome for fuel. Later in the summer Charles Lindbergh, four years after his solo flight across the Atlantic in the *Spirit of St. Louis*, stopped at Nome on a flight from the United States to Asia.

Lindbergh was a consultant for Pan American Airways and was flying the Arctic Circle route from New York to Tokyo with his wife Anne Morrow Lindbergh. She wrote a famous book about their flight called *North to the Orient*. The Lindberghs told the people of Nome "that some day in the very near future they would not be surprised to see large international planes coming and going through Nome to and from the Orient."

The local chamber of commerce claimed in 1931 that Nome was "the logical strategic air base for world and Oriental air transportation."[5]

A U.S. flight crew in front of a Bell Air Cobra. The coming of World War II breathed new life into the city. (Christiansen Collection, University of Alaska Archives)

Nome never became a center for worldwide air traffic, but it was a major stop on Alaskan air routes. By 1939 five major airplane companies operated year-round in Nome, including Wien Alaska Airlines, Mirow Air Service, Ferguson Airways, Northern Cross, and a subsidiary of Pan American, Pacific Alaska Airways.[6]

For many years Pan American, famous for its transoceanic flights, was the most important airline in Alaska. The company had first worked out the techniques for flights across the Atlantic in the Caribbean with short runs from one island to the next, and hoped to develop similiar expertise in its "Alaskan laboratory." In addition to providing service to air-minded Alaskans, they believed their trans-Alaskan service would be the beginning of a major network of round-the-world flights through the Arctic.[7] One of the company's major Alaskan routes in the 1930s was from Fairbanks to Nome.

In 1938 PAA had two flights a week from Fairbanks to Nome, and the price of a ticket for the three-and-a-half-hour trip was $78. After PAA established regular service between southeastern Alaska and Seattle in 1940 with 32-passenger flying boats, Nome was only 15 hours by air from Seattle. With connecting flights on United Airlines regular and sleeper service, the old gold rush town was suddenly only 20 hours from San Francisco, 29 hours from Chicago, and 33 hours from New York.[8]

The airplane had been a curiosity in World War I, flying above the battles in the muddy trenches, but in World War II air power was to be a decisive factor in the outcome. To win the war air superiority became essential, and Alaska was destined to become a battleground.

The territory of Alaska was virtually defenseless in the 1930s. For many years Alaskan politicians had warned of the Japanese threat to America's "Achilles heel," but no one listened. In 1939 the only military base in Alaska was an antiquated post with a few hundred troops in southeastern Alaska, which was leftover from the gold rush.

Front Street during World War II. (University of Alaska Archives)

If it was true that the shortest airline routes to the Orient were through Alaska, it was equally true that a logical route for a Japanese invasion of the United States could be through Fairbanks or Nome. If the Japanese established a base in Alaska, their bombers would only be a few hours away from vital defense industries like the Boeing plant or the Bremerton navy yard near Seattle. On September 1, 1939, Adolf Hitler attacked Poland, and two days later Britain and France declared war on Nazi Germany. After the so-called phony war in the winter of 1939-40, the Germans invaded Norway and Denmark in April 1940, and worried American leaders immediately began a massive military build-up. It took Hitler less than three months to conquer Norway, and amid the growing fear that the United States would be dragged into the war, Congess quickly appropriated funds for the fortification of Alaska. One of the new defense bases was to be located near Nome.

In the summer of 1940 Nome had had a war scare of its own. Rumors spread that the Russians were building a large air and submarine base on Big Diomede Island, only about 150 miles northwest of Nome. The story was not true, but it helped speed through an appropriation of about $350 million for military defense in Alaska.[9]

The construction of the Nome air base began in the summer of 1941. The estimated total cost of the project was about $7 million. "It was realized that Nome's position in relation to global routes of air travel was of great importance," a classified report on Alaska military construction stated in 1944, "and establishment there of a bomber operating base would enable long range patrolling of the Bering Sea and protection of Alaska's west coast. In addition the Nome project was to provide an air base with maximum facilities for medium bombardment and fighter squadrons."[10]

The military facilities at Nome were literally built on the debris left behind by the gold dredges. The tailing piles provided a firm foundation for construction, because the ground was thawed and well drained, even though fields of rock were not the most colorful place for soldiers to live and work. "This is a ground bled dry by the gold mine dredges, which leave nothing but white rocks — tailings," war correspondent Howard Handleman wrote. "The Nome garrison is built on tailings. Every road is solid with tailings. Every Quonset hut and building is on a foundation of tailings. Nowhere in Alaska or the Aleutians is there a post with such a firm foundation."[11]

The base was located on the outskirts of Nome, just across the Snake River, where in 1941 the CAA had built an east-west and a north-south runway. Both of these were relatively short. A longer runway, which was eventually lengthened to nearly eight thousand feet, was built a few miles farther out of town in a huge field of tailings near Anvil Mountain, and became known as the Satellite Field.

A garrison of several hundred men was established at Nome to protect the airstrip, but the facilities were still under construction on December 7, 1941. For the first few days after the attack on Pearl Harbor, the fear in Nome, as elsewhere in Alaska and all along the west coast of the United States, was that the Japanese might strike at any moment. Blackouts and air raid drills were practiced, and guards were posted around the clock at communication facilities to prevent sabotage. Orders were given in Nome explaining how the city should be evacuated in case the need arose. The Nome civilian defense committee helped construct the first radio station in Nome, WXLN, to alert the city in the event of a Japanese attack. Connected to the city's power system, the station was designed to function as an aircraft warning device. The people of Nome tuned in regularly to listen for the alarm. "For filler," a description of the station explained, "phonograph records of pre-World War I vintage, donated by townspeople were offered with heart-breaking regularity, intermingled with instructions on extinguishing incendiary bombs. It was questionable which provided the better entertainment."[12]

In the dark months after Pearl Harbor the war news

in the Pacific was gloomy, as the Japanese followed one stunning success with another. In April 1942, however, 16 American B-25s made a daring daylight bombing raid on Tokyo, proving for the first time to the Japanese people and the rest of the world that the land of the rising sun was not invincible. The leader of this near suicide mission was Lt. Col. James Doolittle, who had come to Nome with his parents as a baby during the great stampede of 1900, and had lived in the city until he was 11 years old. "NOME TOWN BOY MAKES GOOD," said a headline in the *Nome Nugget,* a paper which Doolittle used to deliver as a child. Doolittle attended school in Nome until he moved south with his mother to California in 1908, where the young daredevil later became a champion amateur boxer and a world-famous pilot. He is best remembered today as the leader of Doolittle's Raiders, and the people of Alaska have always been proud that the man who struck the first blow in revenge for Pearl Harbor had grown up in Nome.[13]

Doolittle's daring raid on Tokyo set the stage for the battle of Midway six weeks later in June 1942, the first major Japanese defeat in World War II. The battle brought Nome closer than ever to an actual combat zone. Part of the Japanese strategy at Midway was to divert the American fleet to Alaska. The Japanese bombed Dutch Harbor, and captured Kiska and Attu islands in the Aleutian Chain, making it appear that they were about to invade Alaska, while their real target was farther south at Midway. The diversion toward Alaska did not succeed and many historians now see the Japanese defeat at Midway as the turning point in the war in the Pacific. This was not so clear in 1942, and the weeks following the battle of Midway were the worst of the war for the people of Nome. It was feared that the Japanese would attempt to follow up their successful occupation of Kiska and Attu with an invasion of the Alaska mainland, probably landing somewhere on the Seward Peninsula. On June 20, 1942, intelligence experts

alerted Alaska military officials that the Japanese were about to attack Nome.

The rush to send troops, weapons, and supplies to reinforce Nome in June 1942, has been called the "first mass airlift in American military history."[14] The Alaska Defense Command, under Gen. Simon Bolivar Buckner, called it Operation Bingo. The military commandeered every civilian aircraft possible in Alaska, as well as all available military planes, to begin ferrying supplies to Nome. In about 24 hours a strange armada of 55 aircraft, including cargo planes, passenger liners, and ancient bush planes, flew a total of 179 trips, carrying nearly 2300 men, 20 antiaircraft guns, and tons of supplies to Nome. The troops on the planes were combat ready, prepared to start shooting once they landed at Nome. They carried enough ammunition for 3 days and food for 10.

The threat of an invasion at Nome turned out to be a false alarm, and Japanese troops never came ashore on the Nome beach. The Nome airlift however, continued for about three weeks until the danger passed, and transported altogether nearly 900,000 pounds of men and equipment to fortify the city against the Japanese. Brian Garfield, the leading historian of World War II in Alaska, has said that Operation Bingo was so successful that the Nome airlift was the prototype for the Berlin airlift in 1948.[15]

Probably the most famous outfit stationed in Nome during the war was the Pink Elephant Squadron. The 404th Bombardment Squadron had eight B-24D Liberator bombers, which had been painted pink to camouflage them in the desert sun. Originally destined for Africa, the Pink Elephants were rushed instead to Nome to patrol the Bering Sea. Though the pink bombers were soon repainted dull brown, the official insignia on each plane in the outfit became a flying elephant with flapping ears, which had 20mm guns for tusks, wore goggles, and carried a bomb in its mouth.[16]

An airman and a B-17 bomber on the Nome Air Base. (Christiansen Collection, University of Alaska Archives)

Nome was a key stop on the lend-lease route to Siberia, and had a large complement of Russian military men. (Christiansen Collection, University of Alaska Archives)

Better adapted to Alaskan conditions was the Alaska Territorial Guard. The ATG was an irregular four-thousand-man tundra army largely made up of Eskimos equipped with World War I rifles, who defended Alaskan shores from invasion, infiltration, and sabotage during World War II. The western organizer of the ATG was Marvin ("Muktuk") Marston, who made his headquarters at Nome. Like any guerilla army the ATG traveled faster and lighter than ordinary military scouts, and was intended to provide an effective reconnaissance screen against Japanese attack.[17]

Nome, because of its location, also served as a lend-lease base during the war years. The city was a key stop on the route over which bombers and fighters were ferried to the Soviet Union. Lend-lease was one of the most important Allied strategies during World War II and was designed to utilize the might of the American industrial machine as effectively as possible. The United States provided all of its allies with guns and war material, but was especially eager to keep the Soviet Union in the war against the Nazis. The Russian forces on the eastern front were facing the brunt of the German war machine, and a steady stream of supplies and equipment was sent from the United States to bolster the Soviet armies. The Soviet Union was desperately short of aircraft, and it was decided after long negotiations that the safest way to deliver the bombers and fighters to the Soviet Union would be to fly them through Alaska and Siberia, a route that was called ALSIB.

American pilots flew these lend-lease airplanes north from Great Falls, Montana. The ferry pilots flew along a string of recently completed airfields inland across Canada and northwest to Fairbanks and Nome, but the Soviets would not allow the American airmen to cross over into Siberia. Though Nome was the last ALSIB airfield on American soil, military planners thought it was too vulnerable to Japanese attack, so they chose Fairbanks as the turnover point, where Russian crews replaced Americans, and where the airplanes were

An American flier and nine of his Soviet comrades in Nome.
(Christiansen Collection, University of Alaska Archives)

repainted with the red star of the Soviet Union. By the end of the war nearly seven thousand planes had been delivered to the Russians through Fairbanks and Nome.[18]

The Russian military men and pilots who came through Nome were a group of battle-scarred veterans, many of whom had survived the slaughter on the eastern front. Most of their American counterparts had never been in combat. The Russians enjoyed the little things like

A Hitler impersonator at a wartime variety show in Nome.
(Christiansen Collection, University of Alaska Archives)

shopping in the stores in Nome and Fairbanks for candy and presents, loading up their pockets with all they could carry for the trip back across Siberia, playing pool at the officers' club, or eating a bowl of chocolate ice cream.

The Russians were only too glad to be in Alaska, far from the eastern front, but Americans tended to gripe and complain about being stationed in Nome.

"We thought Cold Bay was tough," Brig. Gen. Edwin Jones said after supervising the construction of the Nome garrison, "but it was lovely compared to this. Those winds come howling off the Bering Straits all winter, and it's cold, bitter cold. The men had to build up the garrison during the winter last year, and I honestly don't know how they could stand it, working out there."[19]

The soldiers stationed in Nome had several choices of entertainment. The troops could listen to WXLN, the Nome radio station that had started in 1941 as an aircraft warning system. Eventually WXLN became a full-fledged radio station with regular programs that the GIs enjoyed, such as "Jivin' With Georgia" and "Reveille Without Beverly." One of the soldiers stationed at Nome was a former co-writer of Bing Crosby's network radio program, and for Christmas 1943 Crosby and the full cast of the Kraft Music Hall put on a specially produced show solely for the soldiers and civilians at Nome.[20]

Though the gold rush saloons like the Northern and the Second Class had long since disappeared, the wartime saloons like the Nevada, the Polar Bar, and May's Tavern were just as crowded as their predecessors had been 40 years earlier. To maintain order only a limited number of soldiers were allowed into Nome at any one time, and while they enjoyed their recreation, military policemen patrolled the streets. Members of a bomber crew stationed in Nome during the big airlift in 1942 were surprised to find that they could buy a steak dinner for $2.50 "served in the quiet and restful atmosphere of the Polar Bar Grill." The airmen found the saloons in Nome to their liking. "Good whiskey is very reasonable," a man in the squadron wrote on June 28, 1942, "and the assortment could be considered a minor miracle considering the difficulty of shipping such items from the states. There were many new and surprising things to be seen in Nome. Nome is proud of its boast that a greater tonnage of liquor is shipped in to their post each year than food (rumor)."[21]

Since Alaska was a combat zone all of the communities in the territory were subjected to the stern measures that might be expected near a battlefront. All travel was subject to approval by the military, and all mail was censored. After the outbreak of the war it was decided that the federal government would stockpile a year's supply of food in various isolated communities throughout the territory in case Japanese submarines were able to control the shipping lanes to Alaska. Until the Japanese were driven from the Aleutians in the late summer of 1943, the danger of starvation was especially great in Nome, which depended so heavily on the food carried in by ship during the open season. The Nome

stockpile in the spring of 1943 included 162 tons of butter, 13 tons of toilet paper, 62 tons of coffee, 420 tons of milk, 32 tons of soap, and 25 tons of dried eggs.[22]

The transition to peacetime after the war was over may have been as difficult in Nome as any place in the country. Social problems erupted during the war in Nome, as in many other American cities, and not all of these problems disappeared when peace was declared in 1945. Founded by gold miners, Nome had largely been a white man's town, and with the growing number of Natives who moved to the city during the war, serious tensions arose. For many years the Eskimos from King Island, the Diomedes, and from all across northwestern Alaska had come to Nome in skin boats during the summertime. Father Bellarmine Lafortune, who had first arrived in Nome in 1903 and was a missionary among the King Island Eskimos for many years, had long been afraid that the white man's way of life would destroy the Eskimos and their culture. As early as 1926 he had proposed that the Eskimos living in Nome should leave

Supplying Nome was especially difficult during the war, with a Japanese threat in the sea lanes in addition to the normal hazards of navigating through the ice. Shown here is the Crown City, *stuck in the ice near Sledge Island.* (Christiansen Collection, University of Alaska Archives)

Nome's controversial segregated movie house, the Dream Theatre.
(Lomen Collection, University of Alaska Archives)

the city and establish a new settlement of their own at Cape Woolley, 37 miles northwest of Nome.[23] Though nothing ever came of the plan, he remained convinced that segregating the Eskimos from the Babylon of Nome would be their only salvation.

During the war years many Eskimos moved permanently to Nome to take jobs in the city, while others went into the service. Father Lafortune was more disturbed than ever at what he saw taking place.

"Booze and loose soldiers are the curse of Nome," Lafortune wrote in 1944. "There is an atmosphere of irreligion all over. It is a poisonous atmosphere that renders even our white and Eskimo Catholics partly paralyzed (spirtually)."[24] This clash between the whites and the Eskimos, who today make up nearly two-thirds of the population of the city, was symbolized by the dispute over separate seating for whites and Eskimos in Nome's only movie house, the Dream Theater.

Eskimos were said to have "complete equality" with whites in Nome except at the hotel and the movie theater. "They can't live at the hotel," a war correspondent wrote in 1943, "and they have to sit on their own side of the theater."[25] Alberta Schenck, a half-Eskimo high school girl, wrote a school paper that was published in the *Nome Nugget* asking why Eskimos had to sit together on one side of the theater. She was an usher at the theater and had to make sure that no Eskimos sat on the wrong side. About a week later she went out on a date with a white sergeant who was stationed at the Nome garrison. The soldier purchased two tickets and walked with Miss Schenck to the white section of the theater. Immediately the manager of the theater asked her to move, but the sergeant insisted that she stay put. The manager called the chief of police who evicted her from the premises and she had to spend the night in jail. After a threat of lawsuits and other action, Miss Schenck appealed to territorial governor Ernest Gruening. The mayor of Nome assured the governor that such an incident would not happen again. Opinions were inflamed over the case both pro and con, but the popular feeling was demonstrated several weeks later in the annual election to pick the queen of the city. Largely with the support of the soldiers of the Nome garrison, Alberta Schenck was elected the Queen of Nome for 1944.[26]

During and after the war, Nome was battered by destructive storms, which seemed almost to follow one after another. The city was ravaged by October storms in 1945 and 1946 which were so destructive that many Nome residents wanted to abandon the city and build a new town farther inland away from the sea. By 1946, Nome had been struck by a succession of four major storms in 1937, 1942, 1945, and 1946, as well as continual minor storms which altogether caused a total of about $3 million in damage.[27]

The 1945 storm hit the city with winds gusting up to 65 miles an hour and towering waves which "tore out waterfront bulkheads like matchsticks."[28] The surf smashed the city with cakes of ice and the Lincoln Hotel broke in two, with the rear half being washed out to sea. In the 1946 storm exactly one year later, the waves blasted the bulkhead and rose 40 to 50 feet in the air, finishing the destruction of the Lincoln Hotel. Two men were killed, six business buildings were leveled, and a dozen others were seriously damaged. "Well, she seems to be dying out," Carl Lomen wrote at half past two on Sunday afternoon, October 27, 1946. "I figure it is the most severe blow Nome has experienced since 1913."[29]

The worst destruction was on the south side of Front Street along the waterfront, where the finest buildings in Nome were located. Since the gold rush the choicest building sites in Nome had been the lots on the south side of Front Street, because the ground near the waterfront was not a frozen mass of ice like the rest of the city. One of the biggest buildings along the waterfront was the Miners and Merchants Bank. Grant Jackson, the president of the bank, explained that there were three main reasons why the south side of Front Street was the site of most of the substantial buildings in Nome, including

Nome's city hall. "You could obtain a good foundation; secure running water from wells; and you could dispose of your sewage," Jackson said. "None of these things were obtainable on the north side of Front Street, where the ground was frozen, without an enormous installation and continuous upkeep expense, if then."[30]

Sand or gravel, which could be found along the waterfront or in a field of tailings, provided an excellent foundation for construction, because the well-drained, thawed ground held little water or ice. Only along the waterfront could buildings with basements, permanent foundations, and modern sanitary facilities be readily constructed in the city of Nome.

Since 1900 storms had regularly damaged or destroyed any structures located near the waterfront, but because the ground was thawed, the south side of Front Street remained the most valuable property in Nome. After the 1934 fire many property owners and taxpayers in Nome had urged that all private property south of Front Street be condemned so that "an engineered sea wall, artificial

A washed out bulkhead along the Nome waterfront in October 1945. (Anchorage Historical and Fine Arts Museum)

Anchorage Historical and Fine Arts Museum

Oliver Jones, Coast Guard Museum

THE LIFESAVING STATION

*O*ver the years the U.S. Life Saving Service and the U.S. Coast Guard have saved many lives in the rough waters of the Nome roadstead. **Upper left** — Breakers smashing a loose lighter on the Nome waterfront. **Lower left** — A Coast Guard crew at Nome, nearly standing at attention. **Right** — Life Saving crew rowing through the breakers to the disabled sloop Greyhound. **Below** — The Life Saving Station on the waterfront, with the boat inside ready for action.

Denny Collection, University of Alaska Archives

Anchorage Historical and Fine Arts Museum

beach or breakwater" could be constructed. The owners of most of the businesses along the waterfront opposed the plan. Each proceeded to build their own bulkheads "according to the ideas and affluence of the property owner." This wall of sand-filled barrels, beach logs, steel pilings, and timbers was not effective protection against the storms of the Bering Sea. "Their weakness somewhat reflected the attitude of their designers," a report stated after the storms of 1946. "They so differed from each other that they did not present a united front against the sea. . . . The continuous erosion so undermined these defenses that they are no longer considered adequate, even by their designers."[31]

With each storm more of the Nome waterfront eroded away. Many businessmen were convinced that the jetties built by the U.S. Army Corps of Engineers at the mouth of the Snake River to provide an entrance to the small-boat harbor had changed the currents along the shore, so that the waves of each storm were progressively destroying the heart of the city. "Obviously unless something is done to prevent it," a breakwater study explained in 1947, "the whole area will be washed away and Nome, one of the most famous cities in the world, for its size, will have been eliminated."[32]

One solution that many residents favored was to move the town away from the sea. A spot under consideration was the Satellite Field, which the army had constructed near Anvil Mountain during World War II. On the thick bed of tailings at the Satellite Field, the new city would not only be safe from Bering Sea storms, but would also be able for the first time to have a city-wide water and sewer system. About two hundred people attended a town meeting at the high school gym in November 1946 to discuss what should be done.

"We must ask the government for assistance," Fr. Edmund Anable of Saint Joseph's Catholic Church said, "but first we must know what we are asking for. We have no sewers, nor adequate drainage, but we do have forests of rusty smoke pipes, little or no fire protection, muddy streets, swamp holes in all parts of town, and very unhealthy and unsanitary conditions."

"I, for one," Father Anable told the crowd of his friends and neighbors, "am in favor of a move toward better living."

Dan Jones, the son of Charlie Jones, a pioneer who had lived in Nome since 1900, was even more emphatic. "I was born here," Jones said. "Even a hole looks good to you if you live in it long enough. If for the convenience of water, sewage disposal, health, and sanitary conditions, I would favor moving to the satellite field."[33]

Dan Jones's sentiments were widely shared. At the end of the meeting a vote was held, and 44 Nome residents favored moving the city, while only 19 were opposed.

The leading businessmen of Nome, including Grant R. Jackson of the Miners and Merchants Bank, the Lomen family, and others, strongly opposed the idea of moving the city. "None of them had the slightest idea of the cost of such a move, what they would have when they got there, and where the money was coming from to make the move," banker Jackson said. "I considered that suggestion fantastic."[34]

Instead of moving the city away from the coast, Jackson and Carl Lomen waged a crusade to build a granite wall between Nome and the Bering Sea. They lobbied for nearly two full years before Congress appropriated about $1 million in 1949 to build a granite sea wall at Nome. The 3,350-foot-long rock wall was completed in 1951. A total of 135,000 tons of rock were trucked in from Cape Nome to build the great wall of Nome, and many of the individual rocks along the top of the wall weighed nearly two tons apiece.[35]

One of the justifications for the construction of the million-dollar sea wall was that the United States had to protect the military base at Nome, which had been named Marks Air Force Base in honor of Maj. Jack S. Marks, who had been shot down and killed over Kiska Island in 1942. During World War II the Nome air base had been the scene of close Russian-American coopera-

The million-dollar granite sea wall built to protect Nome from the Bering Sea. (Fairbanks Daily News-Miner)

tion, but by the late 1940s, Marks Air Force Base was on the front line of the new cold war between the United States and the Soviet Union.

"The people of Nome and northwestern Alaska realize they are in a perilous position," Alaska bush pilot Frank Whaley said in 1948. "Airplanes from Siberia can be over Nome in six minutes."[36] Some politicians believed that the Soviets had a network of spies in northwestern Alaska who were gathering information about American defenses in the region. A congressional committee visited Alaska in 1948 and allegedly "found concrete evidence in Nome that the Soviets are operating a highly-trained espionage system in the far northern regions of the Territory." Representative Charles Kersten of Wisconsin was certain that the Soviets had an active underground in Nome, and he pointed out "that several residents of the northwestern Alaska town subscribe to such publications as *Pravda*, official Moscow newspaper, *Soviet Russia Today, The Daily Worker*, and other American Communist publications."[37]

Fears of the red menace were hardly abated by the decision of the defense department to reduce the military force at Nome in 1949 and 1950 to caretaker status. The startling announcement was made that if Nome was attacked, it would not be defended by United States military forces. The basic strategy for the defense of Alaska shifted dramatically after the Soviet Union exploded its first atomic bomb in 1949. Most of the isolated military installations that had been built in western Alaska and the Aleutians were greatly reduced in strength or abandoned, and forces were concentrated at three air bases near Anchorage and Fairbanks. The major goal of the armed forces in Alaska was to maintain control of the air and to defend the heartland of Alaska between Anchorage and Fairbanks.[38]

Front Street in the mid-1970s. (Fairbanks Daily News-Miner)

Nome today is not the wild town of 1900. But even the early days were not always hectic, and sometimes there was a quiet moment on the waterfront.
(Anchorage Historical and Fine Arts Museum)

"In case of attack...," an article in the *New York Times* explained in 1951, "no effort would be made to defend Nome and the Seward Peninsula. Presumably, the population of some 1,800 would be evacuated by air."[39]

The military build-up across Alaska during the postwar years and the cold war, in accord with this new strategy, had far less of an impact on Nome than on Fairbanks and Anchorage. Until the oil boom started in the late 1960s, military defense remained the single most important industry in Alaska, and the huge air bases near Anchorage and Fairbanks helped transform those cities into the largest in Alaska. While communities in the heartland between Anchorage and Fairbanks have grown dramatically since the war, Nome's population has only increased slightly. The city today is about the same size that it was 70 years ago. Marks Air Force Base shut

176

down in about 1955, and two years later the old air base became the home of Nome's municipal airport.[40]

Even after Alaska became the 49th state in the Union in 1959, the sewage in Alaska's most famous gold rush city was still collected by honey bucket as it had always been, because ordinary water and sewer lines could not be constructed in frozen ground. The issue came up for a vote in 1963, when the people of Nome were asked to approve a bond to pay their share of a million-dollar sewer and water system to be built in a utilidor, especially engineered for permafrost.

"It is nothing short of a miracle that all the people of Nome have not died with such a system we now are operating," Pearse Walsh said in 1963, urging everyone to vote for the bond issue. "It is grossly unsanitary, and truly most deplorable."[41] The measure passed by an overwhelming margin, and after the system was built in mid-1960s, many of the residents of Nome were able to enjoy the luxury of hot and cold running water, and flush toilets, for the first time.

Nome today is the center for transportation, commerce, and government administration in northwestern Alaska. It is a city that still has a large number of saloons along Front Street, as it did during the gold rush, but the street is now straight and wide, and is no longer paved with wood. The population of the city is expected to more than double to about seven thousand people by the end of the 1980s.[42]

The events of recent years and plans for the future repeat many of the concerns of the past. One modern scheme on the drawing board was a deep-water port facility that was planned to be built about three thousand feet offshore, and connected to Nome by a long causeway. The offshore dock would enable large seagoing barges to unload directly to vehicles on the causeway, and eliminate the huge expense of lightering goods ashore, which is still one of the major problems that the city faces today.[43]

Mining is also making a comeback. The last dredges of the U.S.S.R.&M. Co. in Nome shut down in 1962. At that time gold mining was caught in a classic squeeze. While the price of gold remained frozen by the government at $35 an ounce, the cost of operating a dredge continued to rise. Eventually large-scale gold mining was no longer profitable, and it virtually disappeared throughout Alaska by the late 1960s. In the mid-1970s the price of gold was deregulated, and gold mining started to make a comeback. The Alaska Gold Company, a descendant of the old U.S.S.R.&M. Co., owns about 17,000 acres in the Nome area, and began dredging again at Nome in 1975. It is estimated that the company's property still contains at least 1.2 million ounces of gold, enough to keep its dredges operating profitably for another 30 years.[44] Investigations into the practicality of underwater mining in the Bering Sea have continued through the years, as well as preliminary studies for offshore oil development. During the summer of 1981 a headline from the *Nome Nugget* read, " 'Monster' dredge to roam Nome beaches in search of gold." The article described a huge machine with eight rubber wheels each 10 feet tall, which would be driven into the surf to mine the golden sands, much like the Rube Goldberg machines built in 1900 had tried to do.[45]

A more disturbing reminder of Nome's turbulent past was the storm that struck the city on November 11 and 12, 1974. If it had not been for the sea wall the entire town might have been washed off the face of the earth, but even with the sea wall for protection, the early damage estimates ran as high as $30 million. Old-timers believed it was worse than the storm of 1913, the standard by which all previous storms had been judged, and even more destructive than the holocaust of 1934.[46]

The people of Nome rebuilt their city after the 1974 storm as they had done after countless other disasters in the past. Though there really is no logical reason why Nome has survived at the mouth of the Snake River since 1898, it is a safe bet that after the next big storm strikes, the city will rise once again.

NOTES

INTRODUCTION

1. *Seattle Post-Intelligencer,* May 9, 1900; the most detailed treatment of the Nome gold rush is Terrence Cole's "A History of the Nome Gold Rush: The Poor Man's Paradise" (Ph.D. Diss., Univ. of Washington, 1983), from which parts of this account have been drawn.

CHAPTER ONE — THREE LUCKY SWEDES

1. *Seattle Post-Intelligencer,* July 17, 1900.
2. Ibid.
3. Corday MacKay, "The Collins Overland Telegraph," *The British Columbia History Quarterly* 10 (July 1946): 192.
4. Report of Daniel Libby to Charles S. Bulkey, June 20, 1867, Bulkley Collection, Univ. of Washington Manuscript Collection, Seattle, Washington.
5. *Esquimaux,* February 3, 1867.
6. Ibid., January 6, 1867.
7. Libby to Bulkley, June 20, 1867, Bulkley Collection, Univ. of Washington Manuscript Collection.
8. *Esquimaux,* July 7, 1867.
9. U.S. Dept. of Interior, U.S. Geological Survey, *The Gold Placers of Parts of Seward Peninsula, Alaska,* "The Development of the Mining Industry," by Alfred H. Brooks, Bulletin no. 328 (Washington: Government Printing Office, 1908), pp. 13-15.
10. *San Francisco Chronicle,* August 19, 1897.
11. Louis Melsing to "My Darling Sister," September 13, 1897, Libby Collection, Univ. of Alaska Archives, Fairbanks, Alaska.
12. Dorothy Jean Ray, "The Omilak Silver Mine," *The ALASKA JOURNAL®* 4 (Summer 1974): 142-48.
13. *Nome Nugget,* January 1, 1900.
14. N.H. Castle, "A Short History of Council and Cheenik," *The Alaska Pioneer* (June 1912): 8-14; "Council City, Discovery District, Vol. 1, p. 170, Nome Recorder's office, Nome, Alaska.
15. U.S. Dept. of Interior, U.S. Geological Survey, *Past Placer Gold Production from Alaska,* by Philip S. Smith, Bulletin no. 857-B (Washington: Government Printing Office, 1933), p. 96.
16. U.S. Congress. Senate. *History of the Discovery of Gold at Cape Nome,* by H.L. Blake, 56th Cong. 1st sess., S. Doc. 441, pp. 1-2.
17. Ibid.
18. Edward S. Harrison, *Nome and Seward Peninsula* (Seattle: Metropolitan Press, 1905), p. 211.
19. Ibid.
20. Ibid., pp. 210-12; *San Francisco: Its Builders Past and Present,* (San Francisco: Clarke Pub. Co., 1913), pp. 181-83; *Nome Nugget,* January 1, 1900.
21. Harrison, *Nome and Seward Peninsula,* p. 204; Jafet Lindeberg to Frank L. Hess, n.d., in Brooks, "The Development of the Mining Industry," p. 17.
22. Henry Carlisle, "An Interview with Jafet Lindeberg," *Mining Engineering* 16 (July 1964): 112A.
23. Lindeberg to Hess, n.d., in Brooks, "The Development of the Mining Industry," p. 17.
24. Rex Beach, "The Looting of Alaska," *Appleton's Booklovers' Magazine,* January-May 1906 (typescript in Pacific Northwest Collection, Univ. of Washington, Seattle), p. 7.
25. Lindeberg to Hess, n.d., in Brooks, "The Development of the Mining Industry," pp. 17-18.
26. Ibid.
27. U.S. Congress. Senate. *History of the Discovery of Gold at Cape Nome,* p. 9.
28. Harrison, *Nome and Seward Peninsula,* p. 215.
29. Beach, "The Looting of Alaska," p. 9.
30. U.S. Dept. of Labor, *The Yukon and Nome Gold Regions,* by Samuel C. Dunham, Vol. 5, Bulletin no. 29, July 1900, p. 845.
31. Ibid., p. 847.
32. Ibid.; Brooks, "The Development of the Mining Industry," p. 20.
33. Harrison, *Nome and Seward Peninsula,* pp. 51-52; Brooks, "The Development of the Mining Industry," pp. 21-22; Leland H. Carlson, "The First Mining Season at Nome, Alaska-1899," *Pacific Historical Review* 16 (May 1947): 166.
34. Captain E.S. Walker to Major P.H. Ray, July 13, 1899, Patents and Misc. Division: Alaska, Letters Received, 2483-1899, RG 48, National Archives, Washington, D.C.
35. U.S. Congress. Senate. *Report on the Cape Nome Mining Region,* by A.F. Wines, census agent, 56th Cong., 1st sess., S. Doc. 357, May 11, 1900, p. 4.
36. U.S. Dept. of Labor, *The Yukon and Nome Gold Regions,* p. 853.

CHAPTER TWO — THE POOR MAN'S PARADISE

1. *Nome News,* October 9, 1899.
2. Fred R. Cowden, "Historical Paragraphs: Cape Nome Mining District," *The Alaska Pioneer* (June 1913): 9-10.
3. *Seattle Post-Intelligencer,* July 30, 1899; U.S. Congress. Senate. *Report on the Cape Nome Mining Region,* p. 4.
4. George Davidson, "Origin of the Name 'Cape Nome,'" *National Geographic* 12 (November 1901): 398.
5. *Nome Nugget,* September 17, 1901; Harrison, *Nome and Seward Peninsula,* p. 45.
6. Cowden, "Historical Paragraphs," p. 11.
7. *Nome Nugget,* December 20, 1902.
8. U.S. Dept. of Labor, *The Yukon and Nome Gold Regions,* p. 845; Harrison, *Nome and Seward Peninsula,* p. 50.
9. "Nome Location Notices," Vol. 8, March 13, 1899, Nome Recorder's office, Nome, Alaska: *Nome Nugget,* December 20, 1902.
10. *Nome Nugget,* December 20, 1902.
11. Harrison, *Nome and Seward Peninsula,* p. 50.
12. *The Argus* (Seattle), December 23, 1899.
13. The issue of whether or not claims could be staked on the beach became a major battle. For the most part, however, claims were not recognized on the shore. See Brooks, "The Development of the Mining Industry," p. 23.
14. *Seattle Post Intelligencer,* October 15, 1899.
15. Otis E. Young, Jr., *Western Mining* (Norman: University of Oklahoma Press, 1970) pp. 113-14.

16. Ibid.; U.S. Dept. of Interior, U.S. Geological Survey, *Methods and Costs of Gravel and Placer Mining in Alaska,* by C.W. Purington, Bulletin no. 263 (Washington: Government Printing Office, 1905), pp. 55-56; Ernest Wolff, *Handbook for the Alaska Prospector* (College: Mineral Industry Research Laboratory, 1969), pp. 314-15; U.S. Dept. of Interior, U.S. Geological Survey, *Preliminary Report on the Cape Nome Gold Region, Alaska,* by Frank C. Schrader and Alfred H. Brooks (Washington: Government Printing Office, 1900), pp. 29-30.

17. *Nome News,* November 25, 1899: *Seattle Post-Intelligencer,* October 15, 1899.

18. *Seattle Post-Intelligencer,* January 21, 1900.

19. Peter L. Trout, *A New Theory Concerning the Origin and Deposition of Placer Gold* (Seattle: Pigott and French Co. Printers, 1901), p. 79.

20. *Dawson Daily News,* January 21, 1900.

21. Brooks, "The Development of the Mining Industry" p. 25.

22. Forbes Rickard, "Notes on Nome, and the Outlook for Vein Mining in that District," *Engineering and Mining Journal* 71 (March 2, 1901): 275.

23. U.S. Dept. of Interior, U.S. Geological Survey, *Preliminary Report on the Cape Nome Gold Region, Alaska,* p. 22.

24. Ibid., pp. 23-24.

25. U.S. Dept. of Labor, *The Yukon and Nome Gold Regions,* p. 858.

26. Ibid.; U.S. Congress. Senate. *Report on the Cape Nome Mining Region,* pp. 5-7; *Nome News,* October 9, 1899; Brooks, "The Development of the Mining Industry," p. 22.

27. U.S. Dept. of Labor, *The Yukon and Nome Gold Regions,* p. 865.

28. U.S. Congress. Senate. *Report on the Cape Nome Mining Region,* p. 5.

29. Harrison, *Nome and Seward Peninsula,* p. 54.

30. Ibid.

31. U.S. Congress. Senate. *Report on the Cape Nome Mining Region,* p. 10; U.S. Dept. of Labor, *The Yukon and Nome Gold Regions,* pp. 866-87.

32. U.S. Congress. Senate. *Report on the Cape Nome Mining Region,* p. 5.

33. Harrison, *Nome and Seward Peninsula,* p. 55.

34. *Nome News,* March 3, 1900.

35. Harrison, *Nome and Seward Peninsula,* p. 54; U.S. Dept. of Labor, *The Yukon and Nome Gold Regions,* p. 866.

CHAPTER THREE — THE CITY ON THE GOLDEN SAND

1. Allen M. Robinette, *Facts About Cape Nome and Its Golden Sands* (Seattle: Cape Nome Information and Supply Bureau, 1900), p. 2.

2. Brooks, "The Development of the Mining Industry," pp. 22-24.

3. *Klondike Nugget,* January 21, 1900.

4. Edward R. Jesson, "From Dawson to Nome on a Bicycle," *Pacific Northwest Quarterly* 47 (July 1956): 66.

5. Ibid., p. 71.

6. *Nome News,* December 30, 1899.

7. Jesson, "From Dawson to Nome on a Bicycle," p. 74.

8. Ibid.

9. *The Golden Sand of Cape Nome* (St. Paul: Great Northern Railway, 1900).

10. William J. Lampton, "The Cape Nome Gold Fields," *McClure's Magazine* 15 (June 1900): 139.

11. *The Golden Sand of Cape Nome.*

12. Robinette, *Facts About Cape Nome,* pp. 7, 35, 65.

13. *Seattle Post-Intelligencer,* May 14, 1900.

14. Ibid., May 19, 1900; May 21, 1900; May 22, 1900; May 23, 1900; May 26, 1900; May 29, 1900; May 30, 1900; June 24, 1900; June 26, 1900.

15. Ibid., May 21, 1900.

16. Ibid., May 6, 1900.

17. Ibid., May 9, 1900.

18. Diary of Carl Lomen, May 24-25, 1900, Lomen Collection, Univ. of Alaska Archives, Fairbanks, Alaska.

19. Fred Merritt to Mrs. Merritt, May 30, 1900, Merritt Collection, Univ. of Washington Manuscript Collection, Seattle, Washington.

20. "Some Nome Experiences," *Engineering and Mining Journal* 70 (August, 11, 1900): 153.

21. James Galen to "My Dear Sisters," June 9, 1900, Thomas H. Carter Papers, Montana Historical Society Archives, Helena, Montana.

22. Ibid.

23. *Nome News,* May 26, 1900.

24. Ibid.

25. Eugene McElwaine, *The Truth About Alaska: The Golden Land of the Midnight Sun* (Chicago: by the author, 1901), p. 218.

CHAPTER FOUR — ON THE BEACH

1. M. Clark, *Roadhouse Tales or Nome in 1900* (Girard, Kansas: Appeal Publishing Co., 1902), p. 32; *Nome Daily News,* September 12, 1900; *Nome News,* June 23, 1900; G.L. Sheldon, "Reminiscences of the Nome Rush," *Engineering and Mining Journal* 95 (February 1, 1913): 262.

2. *Nome News,* June 23, 1900.

3. See typescript memoir of G.J. Lomen, p. 212, Lomen Collection, Univ. of Alaska Archives, Fairbanks, Alaska.

4. Lanier McKee, *The Land of Nome* (New York: The Grafton Press, 1902), p. 29.

5. Arthur L. Pearse, "Notes on Nome," *Transactions: Institution of Mining and Metallurgy* 9 (February 20, 1901): 181-82.

6. Captain Ellsworth Luce West, *Captain's Papers* (Barre, Massachusetts: Barre Publishers, 1965), p. 81.

7. Charles W. Draper, "Digging Gold on the Seashore," *Metropolitan Magazine* 13 (March 1901): 360.

8. Ibid.

9. Ibid., pp. 360-61.

10. *Seattle Post-Intelligencer,* July 2, 1900.

11. Ibid., July 22, 1900.

12. *Nome Gold Digger,* July 4, 1900.

13. Harrison, *Nome and Seward Peninsula,* p. 58.

14. C.S.A. Frost to the attorney general, August 6, 1900, File 10000/1900, No. 12914/1900, Box 1215, Dept. of Justice, RG 60, National Archives, Washington, D.C.

15. Mary C. Brooke, "The Northern City of Nome," *Independent* 52 (September 20, 1900): 2274.

16. Frost to the attorney general, August 6, 1900, Dept. of Justice, RG 60, National Archives, Washington, D.C.

17. *Nome News,* June 15, 1901.

18. Fred Lockley, *History of the First Free Delivery Service of Mail in Alaska* (Portland: Fred Lockley, 1955).

19. See memoir of John Clum, pp. 29-30, Special Collections, Univ. of Arizona Library, Tucson, Arizona; *Seattle Post-Intelligencer,* July 15, 1900.

20. Lockley, *History of the First Free Delivery of Mail.*

21. *Seattle Post-Intelligencer,* July 2, 1900.

22. *Nome Daily Chronicle,* August 18, 1900.

23. *New York Times,* March 2, 1909.

24. Lucius M. Beebe and Charles Clegg, *San Francisco's Golden Era* (Berkeley: Howell-North, 1962), p. 177: C.B. Glasscock, *Lucky Baldwin* (Indianapolis: Bobbs-Merrill, 1933).

25. *Dawson Daily News,* January 17, 1900.

26. *Nome Daily News,* July 25, 1900.

27. *Nome News,* March 13, 1901.

28. Hal Hoffman, "Cape Nome, Actual Conditions," *Alaskan Magazine* 1 (August 1900): 305.

29. Lockley, *History of the First Free Delivery of Mail.*

30. Elmer Reed, "Letter to the Editor," *Alaska Life* (June 1940): 29.

31. *Nome Gold Digger,* July 4, 1900.

32. U.S. Department of War, "Report of R.G. Ebert, Chief Surgeon," August 29, 1900, Appendix C, Exhibit 4, p. 254, in *Report of Lieut. General Commanding the Army,* Vol. 1, Part 3: "Report of Brig. Gen. George M. Randall, U.S.V., Commanding Dept. of Alaska."

33. Ibid.

34. *Nome Daily News,* June 28, 1900.

35. Quoted in *Engineering and Mining Journal* 69 (July 14, 1900): 46.

36. *Nome Daily News,* June 30, 1900.

CHAPTER FIVE — THE WICKEDEST CITY

1. L.H. French, *Nome Nuggets* (New York: Montross, Clarke and Emmons, 1901), p. 29.

2. *Nome Daily Chronicle,* September 22, 1900.

3. Major P.H. Ray to the commanding officer, Fort Gibbon, November 10, 1899, District of North Alaska-Letters of P.H. Ray, Part 3, Entry 533, RG 393, National Archives, Washington, D.C.

4. Alfred H. Brooks, *Blazing Alaska's Trails* (College: University of Alaska Press, 1973), p. 397.

5. C.S.A. Frost to the attorney general, August 6, 1900, File 10000/1900, No. 12914/1900, Box 1215, Dept. of Justice, RG 60, National Archives, Washington, D.C.

6. *Nome Weekly Chronicle,* October 6, 1900. The figures are slightly different in *Nome Gold Digger,* October 10, 1900.

7. *Nome Daily Chronicle,* September 22, 1900.

8. Glenn G. Boyer, ed., *I Married Wyatt Earp: The Recollections of Josephine Sarah Marcus Earp* (Tucson: University of Arizona Press, 1976), pp. 105-8.

9. *Seattle Post-Intelligencer,* July 22, 1900.

10. *Nome Daily News,* June 29, 1900.

11. Boyer, *I Married Waytt Earp,* pp. 203-4

12. *Arctic Weekly Sun* (Nome), August 5, 1900.

13. *Nome Daily News,* September 12, 1900.

14. *Nome Gold Digger,* September 26, 1900.

15. Ibid., August 1, 1900.

16. *Nome Daily News,* July 31, 1900.

17. Ibid.

18. Ibid.

19. "Police Records of complaints, arrests, charges, and deaths, Nome, 1899-1900," Nome, Alaska, Police Department, 2 vols., Alaska Historical Library, Juneau, Alaska.

20. *Nome Daily News,* July 6, 1900.

21. Ibid.

22. *Nome Daily Chronicle,* August 23, 1900; *Nome Daily News,* August 24, 1900.

23. C.S.A. Frost to C.L. Vawter, August 23, 1900, File 10000/1900, No. 14205/1900, Dept. of Justice, RG 60, National Archives, Washington, D.C.

24. *Nome Chronicle,* June 11, 1901.

25. Fred Merritt to Mrs. Merritt, May 30, 1900, Merritt Collection, Univ. of Washington Archives, Seattle, Washington.

26. *Nome Daily Chronicle,* September 8, 1900.

27. *Nome Daily News,* September 18, 1900.

28. *Nome Daily Chronicle,* September 18, 1900.

29. *The National Cyclopedia of American Biography* (New York: James T. White and Co., 1945), pp. 92-93. The best summary of the controversy is Judge William W. Morrow's article "The Spoilers," *California Law Review* 4 (January 1916).

30. Waldemar E. Lillo, "The Alaska Gold Mining Company and the Cape Nome Conspiracy" (Ph.D. Diss., Univ. of North Dakota, 1935), p. 62.

31. Ibid., p. 230.

32. Morrow, "The Spoilers," pp. 107-8.

33. Lillo, "The Alaska Gold Mining Company and the Cape Nome Conspiracy," p. 230.

34. Rex Reach, "The Looting of Alaska," p. 46.

35. Lillo, "The Alaska Gold Mining Company and the Cape Nome Conspiracy," p. 236.

36. *Nome Gold Digger,* October 17, 1900.

37. *In re* Alexander McKenzie, 180 U.S. 536-551 (1901).

38. Robert P. Wilkins, "Alexander McKenzie and the Politics of Bossism," in *The North Dakota Political Tradition,* ed. Thomas W. Howard (Ames: Iowa State University Press, 1981), p. 21; Lillo, "The Alaska Gold Mining Company and the Cape Nome Conspiracy," p. 273.

39. *In re* Noyes, 121 F. 209 (1902).

40. Lillo, "The Alaska Gold Mining Company and the Cape Nome Conspiracy," p. 329.

41. Morrow, "The Spoilers."

42. Susan H. Johnson, "When Moviemakers Look North," *The ALASKA JOURNAL®* 9 (Winter 1979): 13.

43. U.S. Dept. of Interior, U.S. Geological Survey, *A Reconnaissance of the Cape Nome and Adjacent Gold Fields of Seward Peninsula, Alaska in 1900,* by Alfred H. Brooks, (Washington: Government Printing Office, 1901), p. 69.

44. Pearse, "Notes on Nome," p. 189.

45. *Seattle Post-Intelligencer,* July 22, 1900.

46. *Nome Daily News,* July 12, 1900.

47. *Nome News,* June 23, 1900.

48. *Nome Gold Digger,* July 25, 1900.

49. *Nome News,* June 23, 1900.

50. *Engineering and Mining Journal* 70 (August 25, 1900): 227; U.S. Dept. of Interior, U.S. Geological Survey, *A Reconnaissance of the Cape Nome and Adjacent Gold Fields of Seward Peninsula, Alaska in 1900,* p. 152.

51. *Engineering and Mining Journal* 70 (August 25, 1900): 227.

52. George Wilkinson album, p. 27, Univ. of Alaska Archives, Historical Photograph Collection, Univ. of Alaska, Fairbanks; Thomas R. Rickard, *Through the Yukon and Alaska* (San Francisco: Mining and Scientific Press, 1909), p. 312.

53. *Engineering and Mining Journal* 70 (August 25, 1900): 227.

54. *Nome Gold Digger,* September 19, 1900.

55. *Nome Weekly Chronicle,* October 6, 1900; October 13, 1900: *Nome Gold Digger,* October 10, 1900; U.S. Dept. of War, "Report of the Commissary General," in *Report of the Secretary of War for 1901,* 57th Cong., 1st sess., H. Doc. 2, Vol 1, Part 2, p. 469; *Report of the Secretary of War for 1900,* 56th Cong., 2d sess., H. Doc. 2, Vol. 1, Part 1, pp. 42-43.

56. *Nome Daily News,* August 1, 1900; *Nome Gold Digger,* August 1, 1900; U.S. Dept. of Interior, *Report of the Governor of Alaska,* by John G. Brady, Appendix F (Washington: Government Printing Office, 1900), p. 62.

57. Winthrop Packard, "The Great Storm at Nome," reprinted in *Engineering and Mining Journal* 70 (October 13, 1900): 427.

58. For a general discussion of Alaska's historic population trends, and those of Nome, see Kirk H. Stone, "Populating Alaska: The United States Phase," *The Geographical Review* 42 (July 1952): 384-404. James Ducker's "Gold Rushers to the North: the People of Nome in 1900" (unpublished paper, Alaska Historical Commission, 1982, Anchorage, Alaska) is a fascinating look at the people of Nome as seen through the 1900 census.

CHAPTER SIX — AFTER THE GOLD RUSH

1. Brooks, *Blazing Alaska's Trails,* p. 303.

2. U.S. Dept. of Interior, U.S. Geological Survey, *Past Placer Gold Production from Alaska,* p. 96.

3. U.S. Dept. of Interior, U.S. Geological Survey, *The Gold Placers of Parts of Seward Peninsula, Alaska,* p. 139.

4. *Nome Gold Digger,* November 7, 1900.

5. Ibid., April 10, 1901.

6. For an account of Rickard's career see Charles Samuels, *The Magnificent Rube: Life and Gaudy Times of Tex Rickard* (New York: McGraw Hill, 1957).

7. *Nome Chronicle,* December 29, 1900.

8. Nome City Ordinances, Nos. 22, 36, Polet Collection, Box 1, Univ. of Alaska Archives, Univ. of Alaska, Fairbanks.

9. *Nome Nugget,* December 23, 1907; May 29, 1906.

10. George Avery, "Klondike Mike's Knockout Fight," *The ALASKA SPORTSMAN®,* September 1955, p. 33: Jack Kearns and Oscar Fraley, *The Million Dollar Gate* (New York: Macmillan, 1966).

11. *Nome Daily Chronicle,* August 31, 1900.

12. Ibid., September 5, 1900.

13. *Nome Nugget,* September 24, 1901.

14. *Nome Gold Digger,* August 15, 1900; *Nome Daily Chronicle,* August 13, 1900.

15. *Nome Pioneer Press,* June 3, 1908.

16. *Nome Nugget,* September 16, 1905; September 20, 1905.

17. Ibid., September 13, 1905.

18. Ibid., September 16, 1905.

19. *Nome Pioneer Press,* June 2, 1908; June 3, 1908.

20. Ibid., June 4, 1908.

21. *Nome Gold Digger,* July 2, 1907.

22. *Nome Gold Digger,* July 11, 1900; Dan Dix, "Nome, Metropolis of Northwestern Alaska," *Alaska-Yukon Magazine,* March 1909, pp. 455-58.

23. *Nome Nugget,* May 29, 1906.

24. *Nome Gold Digger,* December 17, 1902.

25. Ibid., December 4, 1901; *Nome Nugget,* November 20, 1901; January 15, 1902; January 22, 1902.

26. *Some Facts About Nome* (Nome, Alaska: Chamber of Commerce, 1907), p. 3.

27. *Nome Daily Chronicle,* September 27, 1900.

28. *Some Facts About Nome* (Nome, Alaska: Chamber of Commerce, 1907), p. 4.

29. *Nome Daily Chronicle,* November 17, 1900.

30. Nome City Ordinances, Nos. 43, 45, Polet Collection, Box 1, Univ. of Alaska Archives.

31. *Nome News,* August 1, 1905.

32. George Wilkinson album, p. 27, Univ. of Alaska Archives, Historical Photograph Collection.

33. *Nome Gold Digger,* September 10, 1902; November 12, 1902; Harrison, *Nome and Seward Peninsula,* pp. 213-14.

34. *Nome News,* October 10, 1905.

35. *Nome Nugget,* October 29, 1956.

36. Evangeline Atwood to Terrence Cole, October 13, 1982.

37. *Nome News,* June 9, 1903.

38. Ibid., July 5, 1900; July 24, 1900; Alice Osborne, "Rails Across the Tundra," *The ALASKA JOURNAL®* 2 (Summer 1972): 2-12; Charles O. Cole, "Gold Rush Railroad," *The ALASKA SPORTSMAN®,* October 1953, p. 12.

39. Osborne, "Rails Across the Tundra," pp. 10-12.

40. *Nome News,* February 24, 1900.

41. *Nome Pioneer Press,* May 16, 1908.

42. Ibid., June 15, 1908.

43. *Nome Gold Digger,* June 22, 1908.

44. *Nome News,* October 13, 1905.

45. *Nome Chronicle,* November 21, 1900.

46. *Nome Gold Digger,* November 21, 1900.

47. Ibid., November 14, 1900.

48. *Nome Chronicle,* February 8, 1901; February 15, 1901.

49. *Nome Nugget,* September 21, 1901.

50. Ibid., April 2, 1902.

51. *Nome Gold Digger,* August 16, 1906.

52. *Nome Nugget,* March 4, 1905.

53. Norm Bolotin, "Nome's 1907 Version of the Globetrotters," *The ALASKA JOURNAL*® 9 (Autumn 1979): 64-67.

54. *Nome Nugget,* December 6, 1902; March 25, 1905; *ALASKA SPORTSMAN*®, December 1968, p. 16.

55. Frank Dufresne, "Dog Mushing in Alaska," *The ALASKA SPORTSMAN*®, March 1936, p. 14. For an account of the founding of the Nome Kennel Club and the All-Alaska Sweepstakes see Scotty Allan's *Gold, Men and Dogs* (New York: G.P. Putnam's Sons, 1931), pp. 176-209. Bill Vaudrin's *Racing Alaskan Sled Dogs* (Anchorage: Alaska Northwest Publishing Co., 1976), contains much information about the present and the past of sled dog racing in Alaska.

56. This and the following quotes about the 1913 storm are from *Nome Nugget,* October 8, 1913.

CHAPTER SEVEN — THE HARDEST YEARS

1. Report of E.D. Evans, acting superintendent of education, June 21, 1919, in Lomen Collection, Box 43, File 629, Univ. of Alaska Archives, Fairbanks, Alaska.

2. Ibid.

3. Flu clippings, Carl Lomen's diary, 1918, in Lomen Collection, Box 20, File 318, Univ. of Alaska Archives, Fairbanks, Alaska.

4. Report of E.D. Evans, June 21, 1919.

5. Ibid.

6. Undated clipping in Nome, Alaska, *Journal,* p. 181, Univ. of Alaska Archives, Vertical File, Fairbanks, Alaska.

7. *Pacific Mining Journal,* December 1912, p. 110.

8. Lillo, "The Alaska Gold Mining Company and the Cape Nome Conspiracy," p. 332.

9. *Who's Who in California 1928/1929,* p. 558.

10. *The Pathfinder,* January 1921, p. 17; *News-Call Bulletin* (California), November 6, 1962.

11. *Alaska Weekly* (Seattle), August 14, 1925.

12. U.S. Dept. of Interior, U.S. Geological Survey, *Past Placer Gold Production from Alaska,* p. 96.

13. The most complete history of dredging in Alaska is John C. Boswell's *History of Alaskan Operations of United States Smelting, Refining and Mining Company* (Fairbanks: Mineral Industries Research Laboratory, 1979). Also see: George J. Young, "California Gold Dredges Go to Nome," *Engineering and Mining Journal-Press,* November 1922, pp. 912-13; Leonard Smith, "History of Dredges in Nome Placer Field," prepared for Hammon Consolidated Gold Fields, Nome, Alaska, March 1926, in Reed Collection, Univ. of Alaska Archives, Fairbanks, Alaska.

14. *Nome Nugget,* January 24, 1925.

15. Ibid., January 31, 1925.

16. *Alaska Weekly* (Seattle), March 20, 1925.

17. *Nome Nugget,* February 21, 1925; Kenneth A. Ungermann, *The Race to Nome* (New York: Harper and Row, 1963), passim.

18. *Alaska Weekly* (Seattle), January 15, 1926.

19. *National Observer,* March 30, 1974; John A. Crawford, "Balto," unpublished manuscript from Cleveland Museum of Natural History, Cleveland, Ohio.

20. Gertrude Ferguson to "Dear Sister," December 29, 1926, Alaska Nurses Collection, Univ. of Alaska Archives, Fairbanks, Alaska.

21. *Nome Nugget,* February 7, 1925; Ungermann, *The Race to Nome,* pp. 160-64 discusses the Togo-Balto controversy. On the suggestion of Carl Lomen, former Alaska governor Thomas Riggs wrote on April 3, 1925, to Francis Gallatin, commissioner of parks in New York City, requesting to no avail that the names of all of the team leaders be carved in the base of the statue in Central Park, thereby acknowledging the effort of the other dogs besides Balto. A copy of Riggs's letter is in the Lomen Collection, Box 9, File 221, Univ. of Alaska Archives.

22. Ibid., September 17, 1901.

23. *Nome News,* May 2, 1905.

24. *Nome Nugget,* May 8, 1911.

25. Ibid., May 10, 1911.

26. Ibid.

27. Ibid., August 28, 1920.

28. Ibid.

29. Ibid.

30. Ibid., August 25, 1923.

31. Ibid., September 15, 1923.

32. Ira Harkey, *Pioneer Bush Pilot: The Story of Noel Wien* (Seattle: University of Washington Press, 1974), p. ix.

33. Ibid., pp. 187-96.

34. Mary Lee Davis, *Uncle Sam's Attic* (Boston: W.A. Wilde Co., 1930), p. 149.

35. *Fairbanks Daily News-Miner,* January 3, 1933.

36. Carl Lomen's *Fifty Years in Alaska* (New York: Mackay, 1954) tells the history of the Lomen family and their experiences with reindeer herding.

37. Richard Stern, " 'I used to have lots of reindeers': the ethnohistory and cultural ecology of reindeer herding in Northwest Alaska" (Ph.D. Diss., SUNY, 1980), p. 123.

38. A. Starker Leopold, *Wildlife in Alaska* (New York: Ronald Press, 1953), p. 69.

39. James and Catherine Brickey, "Reindeer, Cattle of the Arctic," *The ALASKA JOURNAL*® 5 (Winter 1975): 16-24; Leopold, *Wildlife in Alaska,* pp. 68-82.

40. Frank Carpenter, *Alaska: Our Northern Wonderland* (Garden City: Doubleday, 1923), p. 185.

41. Diary of Walter Irwin, 1923, in Lomen Collection, Box 36, File 524, Univ. of Alaska Archives, Fairbanks, Alaska.

42. *Nome, Alaska: Information Concerning Nome and Northwestern Alaska* (Nome: Northwestern Alaska Chamber of Commerce, 1932), p. 4.

43. Ales Hrdlicka, *Alaska Diary 1926-1931* (Lancaster, Pa.: Jaques Cattell Press, 1943), p. 81.

44. Carpenter, *Alaska: Our Northern Wonderland,* p. 186.

45. Diary of Walter Irwin, 1923, Lomen Collection, Box 36, File 524, Univ. of Alaska Archives.

46. *Nome, Alaska: Information Concerning Nome and Northwestern Alaska,* p. 37.

47. Correspondence of Gertrude Ferguson, January 17, 1927, Alaska Nurses Collection, Univ. of Alaska Archives.

48. *Nome Nugget*, September 17, 1969.

49. *Seattle Times*, October 1, 1934.

50. Ibid., September 18, 1934.

51. *The Nome, Alaska, Fire of September 17, 1934: Official Report of Relief Activities of the American Red Cross*, Univ. of Washington, Pacific Northwest Collection pamphlet file.

CHAPTER EIGHT — A TOWN THAT WOULDN'T DIE

1. *Nome Nugget*, October 23, 1934.

2. Ibid., October 15, 1934.

3. Ibid.

4. *Annual Report of the Alaska Road Commission*, 1927, p. 76.

5. *Cordova Daily Times*, "All Alaska Review for 1931," p. 12.

6. *Interesting Facts About Nome* (Nome: Chamber of Commerce, 1939).

7. *Aviation*, August 1934.

8. *Nome Nugget*, June 12, 1940.

9. Brian Garfield, *The Thousand Mile War* (New York: Ballantine Books, 1969), p. 57.

10. James D. Bush, *Narrative Report of Alaska Construction: 1941-1944*, U.S. Army, Construction Division, Alaskan Dept., p. 92.

11. Howard Handleman, "Alaska's Strangest Garrison," *Alaska Life*, April 1944, p. 48.

12. *Alaska Life*, "Voice of the Arctic," May 1945, p. 48.

13. Phyllis D. Carlson, "Jimmy Doolittle," *Take Me Away*, August 1980, pp. 11-13.

14. Garfield, *The Thousand Mile War*, p. 118.

15. Ibid., p. 120.

16. Ibid., p. 121; "Pink Elephants," *Alaska Life*, February 1944, p. 45.

17. Muktuk Marston, *Men of the Tundra: Alaska Eskimos at War* (New York: October House, 1969), passim.

18. Lyman Woodman, "An Alaskan Military History," *ALASKA SPORTSMAN®*, March 1969, p. 22; Otis E. Hays, Jr., "White Star — Red Star," *The ALASKA JOURNAL®* 12 (Summer 1982): 9-17; Deane R. Brandon, "ALSIB: The Northwest Ferrying Route Through Alaska, 1942-45," *American Aviation Historical Society Journal* 20 (Spring-Summer 1975).

19. Handleman, "Alaska's Strangest Garrison," p. 48.

20. *Alaska Life*, "Voice of the Arctic," May 1945, p. 48.

21. Wheeler war diary (photocopy), June 28, 1942, in Brian Garfield Collection, Univ. of Oregon Archives, Eugene, Oregon.

22. Hagerty Report, March 6, 1943, Bartlett Collection, Univ. of Alaska Archives, Fairbanks, Alaska.

23. Louis Renner, *Pioneer Missionary to the Bering Strait Eskimos: Bellarmine Lafortune, S.J.* (Portland: Binford and Mort for the Alaska Historical Commission, 1979), p. 108.

24. Ibid., p. 141.

25. *Alaska Life*, "Wartime Alaska," December 1943, p. 46.

26. Ernest Gruening, *Many Battles: The Autobiography of Ernest Gruening* (New York: Liveright, 1973), p. 321; Marston, *Men of the Tundra*, pp. 130-40; Ernest Gruening to Alberta Schenck, March 17, 1944, Otto Geist Collection, Alaska Territorial Guard Papers, Box 6, Nome Correspondence, Univ. of Alaska Archives, Fairbanks, Alaska.

27. "Report of the Committee on Breakwater," January 13, 1947, Lomen Collection, Box 44, File 635, Univ. of Alaska Archives, Fairbanks, Alaska.

28. *Seattle Times*, October 30, 1945.

29. Memorandum of Carl Lomen, October 27, 1946, Lomen Collection, Box 13, File 285, Univ. of Alaska Archives, Fairbanks, Alaska.

30. Grant Jackson to E.L. ("Bob") Bartlett, January 2, 1947, Lomen Collection, Box 44, File 635, Univ. of Alaska Archives, Fairbanks, Alaska.

31. "Report of the Committee on Breakwater," January 13, 1947, Lomen Collection, Box 44, File 635, Univ. of Alaska Archives.

32. Ibid.

33. *Nome Nugget*, November 25, 1946.

34. Grant Jackson to E.L. ("Bob") Bartlett, January 2, 1947, Lomen Collection, Box 44, File 635, Univ. of Alaska Archives.

35. *Nome Nugget*, December 1, 1950; *Facts About Nome, Alaska* (Nome: Northwestern Alaska Chamber of Commerce, 1960).

36. *Seattle Post-Intelligencer*, March 25, 1948.

37. *Tewkesbury's Alaska Business Directory*, 1950, p. 26.

38. Hanson W. Baldwin, "Alaska: Rampart We Must Watch," *New York Times Magazine*, April 23, 1950.

39. *New York Times*, February 23, 1951.

40. Woodman, "An Alaskan Military History," p. 26; John H. Cloe, command historian, to Terrence Cole, September 28, 1982; Robert E. Frenkel, *Nome, Alaska: A Library Summary*, report prepared for Pacific Missile Range, Point Mugu, California, p. 15.

41. *Nome Nugget*, January 14, 1963; January 23, 1964.

42. Ibid., August 12, 1982.

43. *Nome Nugget*, "Special Historical Edition," n.d.

44. *Fairbanks Daily News-Miner*, July 3, 1975.

45. *Nome Nugget*, July 9, 1981.

46. Ibid., November 22, 1974.

Alaska Geographic® Back Issues

The North Slope, Vol. 1, No. 1. The charter issue of *ALASKA GEOGRAPHIC®*. Out of print.

One Man's Wilderness, Vol. 1, No. 2. The story of a dream shared by many, fulfilled by a few; a man goes into the Bush, builds a cabin and shares his incredible wilderness experience. Color photos. 116 pages, $9.95.

Admiralty . . . Island in Contention, Vol. 1, No. 3. An intimate and multifaceted view of Admiralty; it's geological and historical past, its present-day geography, wildlife and sparse human population. Color photos. 78 pages, $5.00.

Fisheries of the North Pacific: History, Species, Gear & Processes, Vol. 1, No. 4. Out of print. (Book edition available)

The Alaska-Yukon Wild Flowers Guide, Vol. 2, No. 1. Out of print. (Book edition available)

Richard Harrington's Yukon, Vol. 2, No. 2. Out of print.

Prince William Sound, Vol. 2, No. 3. Out of print.

Yakutat: The Turbulent Crescent, Vol. 2, No. 4. Out of print.

Glacier Bay: Old Ice, New Land, Vol. 3, No. 1. The expansive wilderness of southeastern Alaska's Glacier Bay National Monument (recently proclaimed a national park and preserve) unfolds in crisp text and color photographs. Records the flora and fauna of the area, its natural history, with hike and cruise information, plus a large-scale color map. 132 pages, $11.95.

The Land: Eye of the Storm, Vol. 3, No. 2. Out of print.

Richard Harrington's Antarctic, Vol. 3, No. 3. The Canadian photojournalist guides readers through remote and little understood regions of the Antarctic and Subantarctic. More than 200 color photos and a large fold-out map. 104 pages, $8.95.

The Silver Years of the Alaska Canned Salmon Industry: An Album of Historical Photos, Vol. 3, No. 4. Out of print.

Alaska's Volcanoes: Northern Link in the Ring of Fire, Vol. 4, No. 1. Out of print.

The Brooks Range: Environmental Watershed, Vol. 4, No. 2. Out of print.

Kodiak: Island of Change, Vol. 4, No. 3. Out of print.

Wilderness Proposals: Which Way for Alaska's Lands? Vol. 4, No. 4. Out of print.

Cook Inlet Country, Vol. 5, No. 1. Out of print. All-new edition (Vol. 10, No. 2) available.

Southeast: Alaska's Panhandle, Vol. 5, No. 2. Explores southeastern Alaska's maze of fjords and islands, mossy forests and glacier-draped mountains — from Dixon Entrance to Icy Bay, including all of the state's fabled Inside Passage. Along the way are profiles of every town, together with a look at the region's history, economy, people, attractions and future. Includes large fold-out map and seven area maps. 192 pages, $12.95.

Bristol Bay Basin, Vol. 5, No. 3. Out of print.

Alaska Whales and Whaling, Vol. 5, No. 4. The wonders of whales in Alaska — their life cycles, travels and travails — are examined, with an authoritative history of commercial and subsistence whaling in the North. Includes a fold-out poster of 14 major whale species in Alaska in perspective, color photos and illustrations, with historical photos and line drawings. 144 pages, $12.95.

Yukon-Kuskokwim Delta, Vol. 6, No. 1. Out of print.

The Aurora Borealis, Vol. 6, No. 2. The northern lights — in ancient times seen as a dreadful forecast of doom, in modern days an inspiration to countless poets. What causes the aurora, how it works, how and why scientists are studying it today and its implications for our future. 96 pages, $7.95.

Alaska's Native People, Vol. 6, No. 3. Examine the varied worlds of the Inupiat Eskimo, Yup'ik Eskimo, Athabascan, Aleut, Tlingit, Haida and Tsimshian. Included are sensitive, informative articles by Native writers, plus a large, four-color map detailing the Native villages and defining the language areas, 304 pages, $24.95.

The Stikine, Vol. 6, No. 4. River route to three Canadian gold strikes in the 1800s, the Stikine is the largest and most navigable of several rivers that flow from northwestern Canada through southeastern Alaska on their way to the sea. Illustrated with contemporary color photos and historic black-and-white; includes a large fold-out map. 96 pages, $9.95.

Alaska's Great Interior, Vol. 7, No. 1. Alaska's rich Interior country, west from the Alaska-Yukon Territory border and including the huge drainage between the Alaska Range and the Brooks Range, is covered thoroughly. Included are the region's people, communities, history, economy, wilderness areas and wildlife. Illustrated with contemporary color and black-and-white photos. Includes a large fold-out map. 128 pages, $9.95.

A Photographic Geography of Alaska, Vol. 7, No. 2. An overview of the entire state — a visual tour through the six regions of Alaska: Southeast, Southcentral/Gulf Coast, Alaska Peninsula and Aleutians, Bering Sea Coast, Arctic and Interior. Plus a handy appendix of valuable information — "Facts About Alaska." Revised in 1983. Approximately 160 color and black-and-white photos and 35 maps. 192 pages, $15.95.

The Aleutians, Vol. 7, No. 3. Home of the Aleut, a tremendous wildlife spectacle, a major World War II battleground and now the heart of a thriving new commercial fishing industry. Contemporary color and black-and-white photographs, and a large fold-out map. 224 pages, $14.95.

Klondike Lost: A Decade of Photographs by Kinsey & Kinsey, Vol. 7, No. 4. An album of rare photographs and all-new text about the lost Klondike boom town of Grand Forks, second in size only to Dawson during the gold rush. $12.95.

Wrangell-Saint Elias, Vol. 8, No. 1. Mountains, including the continent's second- and fourth-highest peaks, dominate this international wilderness that sweeps from the Wrangell Mountains in Alaska to the southern Saint Elias range in Canada. Includes a large fold-out map. 144 pages, $9.95.

Alaska Mammals, Vol. 8, No. 2. From tiny ground squirrels to the powerful polar bear, and from the tundra to the magnificent whales inhabiting Alaska's waters, this volume includes 80 species of mammals found in Alaska. 184 pages, $12.95.

The Kotzebue Basin, Vol. 8, No. 3. Examines northwestern Alaska's thriving trading area of Kotzebue Sound and the Kobuk and Noatak river basins, lifelines of the region's Inupiat Eskimos, early explorers, and present-day, hardy residents. 184 pages, $12.95.

Alaska National Interest Lands, Vol. 8, No. 4. Following passage of the bill formalizing Alaska's national interest land selections (d-2 lands), longtime Alaskans Celia Hunter and Ginny Wood review each selection, outlining location, size, access, and briefly describing the region's special attractions. 242 pages, $14.95.

Alaska's Glaciers, Vol. 9, No. 1. Examines in depth the massive rivers of ice, their composition, exploration, present-day distribution and scientific significance. 144 pages, $9.95.

Sitka and Its Ocean/Island World, Vol. 9, No. 2. From the elegant capital of Russian America to a beautiful but modern port, Sitka, on Baranof Island, has become a commercial and cultural center for southeastern Alaska. 128 pages, $9.95.

Islands of the Seals: The Pribilofs, Vol. 9, No. 3. Great herds of northern fur seals drew Russians and Aleuts to these remote Bering Sea islands where they founded permanent communities and established a unique international commerce. 128 pages, $9.95.

Alaska's Oil/Gas & Minerals Industry, Vol. 9, No. 4. Experts detail the geological processes and resulting mineral and fossil fuel resources that are now in the forefront of Alaska's economy. Illustrated with historical black-and-white and contemporary color photographs. 216 pages, $12.95.

Adventure Roads North: The Story of the Alaska Highway and Other Roads in The MILEPOST®, Vol. 10, No. 1. From Alaska's first highway — the Richardson — to the famous Alaska Highway, first overland route to the 49th state, text and photos provide a history of Alaska's roads and take a mile-by-mile look at the country they cross. 224 pages, $14.95.

ANCHORAGE and the Cook Inlet Basin, Vol. 10, No. 2. "Anchorage country" . . . the Kenai, the Susitna Valley, and Matanuska. Heavily illustrated in color and including three illustrated maps . . . one an uproarious artist's forecast of "Anchorage 2035." 168 pages, $14.95.

Alaska's Salmon Fisheries, Vol. 10, No. 3. The work of *ALASKA®* magazine Outdoors Editor Jim Rearden, this issue takes a comprehensive look at Alaska's most valuable commercial fishery. 128 pages, $12.95.

Up the Koyukuk, Vol. 10, No. 4. Highlights the Koyukuk region of north-central Alaska . . . the wildlife, fauna, Native culture and more. 152 pages. $14.95.

NEXT ISSUE:
Alaska's Farms and Gardens, Vol. 11, No. 2. An overview of the past, present, and future of agriculture in Alaska, and a wealth of information on how to grow your own fruit and vegetables in the north. To members in May 1984. Price to be announced.

Your $30 membership in the Alaska Geographic Society includes 4 subsequent issues of *ALASKA GEOGRAPHIC®*, the Society's official quarterly. Please add $4 for non-U.S. membership.

Additional membership information available upon request. Single copies of the *ALASKA GEOGRAPHIC®* back issues are also available. When ordering, please add $1 postage/handling per copy. To order back issues send your check or money order and volumes desired to:

The Alaska Geographic Society

Box 4-EEE, Anchorage, AK 99509